"An in-depth read for a new way of contribution to American Buddhist

—NORMAN OBERSTEIN, CEO, Frederick P. Lenz Foundation for American Buddhism

"A practical workbook blending modern psychology with ancient wisdom, *Zen Beyond Mindfulness* leaves a breadcrumb trail to awakening. Dr. Harris clearly has a love affair with truth and the potentiality of human individual evolution. Enlightenment can bang on his door at 3 a.m. and he will always get up and make time."

—DR. CONRAD FISCHER, MD,
Program Director, Brookdale Hospital Medical Center

"Buddhism has a history of adapting to the culture of a country where it is introduced. In the West, that adaptation includes the merging of modern psychology with traditional Buddhism. In *Zen beyond Mindfulness*, Shuzen Harris makes a significant contribution to this dialogue. Shuzen tackles difficult Buddhist subjects with a clarity and writing style that renders them accessible to the reader. He then fuses those subjects with the psychology of I-Systems to help students of Zen dissolve emotional and psychological barriers to deepening their meditation practice. Due to his many years of direct experience, Shuzen brings a profound understanding to both Zen and psychology that makes this book particularly relevant and beneficial."

—GERRY SHISHIN WICK,
author of *The Book of Equanimity: Illuminating Classic Zen Koans*

"*Zen beyond Mindfulness* will enable both new and seasoned practitioners to gain a better understanding of how the mind works. A compelling teaching guide imbued with boundless wisdom and clarity, this book is a twenty-first-century teaching that will stand the test of time!"

—HEILA AND RODNEY DOWNEY,
Guiding Teacher and Abbot of the Dharma Centre,
Cape Town, South Africa

ZEN
BEYOND
MINDFULNESS

USING BUDDHIST AND MODERN PSYCHOLOGY
FOR TRANSFORMATIONAL PRACTICE

. . .

JULES SHUZEN HARRIS

Foreword by Roshi Pat Enkyo O'Hara

SHAMBHALA
BOULDER
2019

Shambhala Publications, Inc.
4720 Walnut Street
Boulder, Colorado 80301
www.shambhala.com

9 8 7 6 5 4 3 2 1

First Edition
Printed in the United States of America

⊗This edition is printed on acid-free paper that meets
the American National Standards Institute Z39.48 Standard.
♻This book is printed on 30% postconsumer recycled paper.
For more information please visit www.shambhala.com.

Shambhala Publications is distributed worldwide
by Penguin Random House, Inc., and its subsidiaries.

Designed by Claudine Mansour Design

Library of Congress Cataloging-in-Publication Data

Names: Harris, Jules (Jules Shuzen), author.
Title: Zen beyond mindfulness: using Buddhist and modern psychology
for transformational practice/Jules Shuzen Harris.
Description: First edition. l Boulder: Shambhala, 2019. l
Includes bibliographical references.
Identifiers: LCCN 2018030019 l ISBN 9781611806625 (pbk.: alk. paper)
Subjects: LCSH: Zen Buddhism—Psychology. l
Meditation—Zen Buddhism. l Zen Buddhism—United States.
Classification: LCC BQ9265.8.H37 2019 l DDC 294.3/44—dc23
LC record available at https://lccn.loc.gov/2018030019

CONTENTS

FOREWORD

By Roshi Pat Enkyo O'Hara

MORE AND MORE of us in the Western world are drawn to finding our way by looking directly at our minds. One method we hear about is the practice of mindfulness and how it can yield powerful gifts—better health, improved concentration, and most importantly, the sense that we are truly present for our lives. And yet, it turns out to not be quite so easy to reap these benefits. Stories, memories, false ideas, and schemes creep into our understanding of who we are and into our life itself. There are, it turns out, many barriers to the insight and ease offered by mindfulness and meditation.

The difficulty of establishing true and consistent mindfulness is not new. An old, much-loved koan tells the story of Zuigan, a Zen master who, every day after rising, would sit down and call out to himself,

"Oh Master!"

And he would answer himself, "Yes?"

And then he would say, "Don't be deceived by anyone, anytime, anyway."

And then he would reply, "No I won't!"

Imagine, before your day begins—even before your mindfulness practice or prayers begin—you interrogate yourself, as Zuigan did, and remind yourself to defend against self-deception. Amazing! Why would anyone do such a thing? Isn't it that, without realizing it, we do deceive ourselves through our desires to see things (other people, situations, our own presentation of "self") in a certain way? And through this lens of our desires, we miss the reality actually in front of us: our life as it is.

What to do about this tendency? How can we achieve the benefits of mindfulness without falling into self-deception? Through the ages, there have been many responses to this need, all well-suited to their times. Today, with the development of psychology and the convergence of many spiritual traditions, a truly useful and effective method of integrating mindfulness meditation into our lives is critically needed.

Jules has developed a skillful and wise method for working with our tendency to distort thinking, so that we don't derail our intentions to practice mindfulness and can stay true to our goal of living a life of awareness and compassion. By folding in the ancient Buddhist teachings on mind (the Abhidharma) with contemporary psychology and Zen rigor, he offers a creative and beneficial system to practice mindfulness with success and integrity. Although the use of "mind maps" will be new to many Zen practitioners, this tool affords a useful corrective for those who find their Zazen stagnating or who want to check their practice of nonattachment against the concrete, bodily evidence made available by the mind mapping exercises.

I've known Jules since his early days in Zen practice. In this book he brings together his years of working as a psychotherapist, as a master of the graceful and disciplined Japanese martial arts of *Kendo* and *Iaido*, and as a Zen teacher in the White Plum Asanga lineage. I can't think of a more qualified and appropriate person to take on the task of developing a contemporary technique for using mindfulness as a path of self-discovery and peace.

I am gratified that he is my Dharma Successor and to see him offering such a useful teaching, grounded as it is in Zen practice.

PREFACE

My Path

I WAS BORN in 1939 in Chester, Pennsylvania, an industrial town just outside of Philadelphia that was working class and extremely diverse. Based on this background, the path I ended up taking was exceedingly unlikely. It was unlikely that I would travel to India, China, Tibet, Egypt, South Africa, and Japan studying different religious traditions and practices. It was unlikely that I would come to study Zen at all, let alone become the first African American man to receive transmission in the Soto Zen school and become a dharma teacher with my own center. But that's what happened.

From the very beginning I was a seeker, always looking up, wondering if there was more than this. My grandmother was a Baptist, and when I was a young boy, she took me to church every Sunday. I found sitting through the long sermons incredibly dull, and I hated sitting still. (The irony of this doesn't escape me.) That branch of Christianity never spoke to me, although one highlight of the Baptist experience was hearing Dr. Martin Luther King Jr. give a sermon. (He was doing his internship at Calvary Baptist while at Crozier Seminary.)

Instead of the Baptist Church, I was drawn first to Catholicism. I took trumpet lessons from nuns and would occasionally go to mass. In this way, I met a Catholic priest who was a former professional basketball player with the Philadelphia Warriors. He impressed me so much that I briefly considered turning my spiritual yearnings toward the priesthood. One day we were discussing St. Thomas Aquinas and his second argument for the existence of God. The priest explained the impossibility of an infinite chain with the standard analogy of dominos. He argued that there could be hundreds of dominos knocked over by pushing the first in line, but all the action of those hundreds of dominos didn't explain who set them up. But I was more interested in the question "Who pushed over the first domino?" He laughed and said I might be better off with Eastern philosophy. I didn't understand him entirely then, but he was right. I've always been much less interested in the existential questions—Is there a God? What is his ultimate plan?—than in the practical questions of how to be a good person and find meaning in the here and now. I don't care who set up all these dominos, but I sure want to know the best way to keep them from falling over and crashing into each other. By the time I was twenty-one, I'd been mentored by Quakers, joined and then left the Nation of Islam, and even considered studying Judaism.

My seeking always had a practical or worldly focus. While studying at Staten Island College, I was part of a program that trained students to be ombudsmen for the community. We developed contacts at various social service agencies, so we could help people get the help they needed: we had contacts in various law offices, in the local clinic, and in different government services. We were there to make it possible for people to navigate the system. This work led me, in Zen terms, to great doubt. Seeing the pain people were in, day after day, and how people abused each other out of fear and anger, I felt I had to understand why people hurt each other so easily and whether there was more to life than just trying to find safety for oneself and one's family. I didn't realize it then, but I was facing the same questions the Buddha faced: Why is there suffering, and is there a way out?

As I struggled with this great doubt, I became more interested in Eastern religions and philosophies. I began to study yoga—not the hatha yoga, the physical postures, that has become familiar to Americans, but *dhyana*, which is absorption meditation. I became interested in the teachings of Kirpal Singh and even went to India to meet with him, arriving just nineteen days before he died. When I returned home, I spent some time with others who followed him by listening to tapes of his talks, but that wasn't what I was looking for—I wanted to engage in discussion with a teacher, not just listen to talks. Eventually, someone in that group told me about Tibetan Buddhism and Chögyam Trungpa Rinpoche, saying that his teachings were the closest thing to the meditations we would do after we listened to Kirpal Singh's talks.

I studied in the Tibetan tradition for a few months, learning from Trungpa Rinpoche and other Tibetan teachers who visited Woodstock, New York. Trungpa Rinpoche wanted his students to experience Zen. I went to a weekend Zen retreat in Vermont, and there I met Taizan Maezumi Roshi. I had an interview with him, and when I met him, I felt I had come home—finally, here was my path. I was so impressed by Maezumi Roshi and especially by his clarity: he had an intense focus and calm that I'd never seen in any teacher before. He had a beautiful kind of joy and was present in every moment. I always say, "His eyes didn't roll back in his head." By that I mean he didn't take drugs or get blissed out on meditation. For him, it was always about being really present and aware, and I admired that immensely. I wanted that for myself, so I knew I had to become his student and study Zen.

In the end, I settled into Zen because, despite its mystical reputation, it is the most practical and hard-nosed of all the religions I encountered. The goal of Zen is always the here and now. Through the ages, Zen teachers have used a variety of methods to impress on their students that what matters is this very moment. Some of the methods seem harsh or even dangerous now—shouting at students or hitting them. Others are almost certainly exaggerations or myths—Master Gutei cutting off his student's finger, Nansen killing a cat in front of his students when none of them could speak a "turning word" (proof that they had fully understood their true nature). But what impressed me is that Zen was always about smacking up against the reality of suffering, not intellectualizing it.

For several years, I studied with John Daido Loori at Mount Tremper. At first, I advanced very quickly; because of all my years in the yogic tradition, I started on koans almost immediately, and I became Daido's right-hand man. I gave talks, was involved in a discussion about setting up a center in New York, and even accompanied Daido on a trip to Japan to meet with Maezumi Roshi. So, at that point, I was fully committed to the practice . . . or so I thought.

The truth is that my practice was suffering. I was focused on my status and not my practice. I wasn't sitting enough; instead, I was caught up in the ego trip of being on the board of directors and helping to run things. As I said, I became Daido's right-hand man. I felt I had arrived, and the external validation helped me believe I was doing Zen "the right way."

I was deeply involved in the organization but not really practicing. Finally, a senior student took me aside and told me that I wasn't sitting enough and that other people who had less experience or who had started after me were surpassing me in terms of clarity and koan practice. It was then that I really understood how central sitting was to the practice and to waking up. In fact, my breakthrough came when I really dedicated myself to sitting. I had been stuck on the koan "Mu" for a long time, and I was frustrated beyond belief. I decided I was going to sit up all night if necessary, until I saw it. And that's when I did pass "Mu"—when I just sat down on the cushion at a weekend *sesshin* and let tiredness and pain overwhelm my defenses and my beliefs about myself and the world. It was my aha moment. It was a feeling of just knowing. It was euphoric and confirming. What this moment confirmed was my belief that this path was the right path for me and that the teachings of the Buddha were the best solution to the inner turmoil and searching I'd experienced my whole life.

Unfortunately for many of us, the stressful life we live, the materialistic preoccupation we have, and the education we receive seldom gives us the freedom to understand our intrinsic nature, which is boundless. This is why the presence of the Buddha and his teachings in our time are so important. We need these teachings to show us the potential that lies hidden within our normal, distressed, neurotic, and busy minds. When we begin to explore through sitting, we inevitably encounter the wild and uncontrollable aspects of our habitual mind. But with some guidance and skillful practice we begin to recognize that the mind has an undercurrent of clarity and luminosity.

Excerpt from "Realizing Your Buddha-Nature"
(Dharma talk given at Soji Zen Center, 2016)

ACKNOWLEDGMENTS

I AM GRATEFUL to many people who helped me with this book. Nine bows to my teachers: Marshall Davis and Roshis John Daido Loori, Dennis Genpo Merzel, and Pat Enkyo O'Hara, who opened my eyes and heart to the dharma. Heartfelt appreciation for Stanley Block, an old friend and mentor, who trained me in the use of the Mind-Body Bridging method and granted me unlimited application. Gratitude to Soji's study group, whose transcriptions of my class lectures and assignments created the framework of the book. Special gratitude to Annalisa Rakugo Castaldo and Brenda Jinshin Waters, who refined my utterances. Thanks to Dermot Genjaku Mac Cormack for his help in creating the mind map figures. To Dave O'Neal and Matthew Zepelin, for their editorial guidance, which helped shape my vision of how this book can help others on their path. A special thanks to the staff at Shambhala Publications who put all of the pieces together. And thanks for everyone who has walked through the door at Soji; for you my practice continues.

Lastly, I thank my wife, Cathy, and son, Shane Kamu, for their unwavering support throughout the project.

—JULES SHUZEN HARRIS

ZEN BEYOND MINDFULNESS

INTRODUCTION

Zen, Abhidharma, and the I-System

WHEN I TOOK the precepts, I was given the name Shuzen, which translates to "Defender of the Practice" or "Protector of the Teachings." I have always taken that name very seriously, and for the last thirty-six years, my life has been focused, in various ways, on preserving, protecting, and passing on the dharma. As I have devoted more of myself to teaching the dharma, I've come to see that my name actually has a dual meaning. I am not only protecting the traditions and passing them on as they were passed on to me but also finding new ways to share the dharma so that it finds root in the twenty-first-century United States. This is a tricky path to walk; it is not easy to determine what the heart of the practice is, what can be modified or discarded without harm, and what should or even *must* be discarded or changed to keep the practice vital.

To take just one example I've grappled with, there's the question of lay priests. For centuries, all Buddhist priests left home, both literally and figuratively, in order to devote themselves exclusively to practice. Furthermore, priests were always male—a woman could become a nun and have a life of practice, but she could not become a priest. To protect the tradition of priesthood in a literal sense would mean ordaining only men, and only those men who were willing to give up their jobs and become residents in a monastery. A very few US monasteries do follow this model, but this is obviously not workable for the majority of centers and practitioners. Most temples and centers in the United States, including my own, are small groups that could not afford to support even a single full-time priest, let alone several. Furthermore, most people who are drawn to the priesthood are like myself in that they have families and jobs before they discover a desire to serve in the role of priest. To keep to the traditional practice would mean almost no American priests.

Another approach would be to do away with the priesthood altogether. This is the choice some American teachers have made. Some teachers who were ordained have disrobed and given up their dharma names because they feel the Japanese element is a barrier that puts off people from exploring Zen; their goal is to make Zen as welcoming as possible to as many people as possible. Many other teachers have chosen not to be formally ordained as priests in the first place. Their groups offer meditation and discussion of modern works about Buddhism but little or no study of the sutras, koan practice, or instruction in the ritual of traditional Zen practice.

In this, as in so many other things, I have chosen to follow a middle path. While I recognize that some prospective students, when they first visit our center (Soji Zen Center, in Lansdowne, Pennsylvania), may be put off by seeing people in robes or by chanting and doing full prostrations, ritual is too important—to me, to the center, and to the lives of my students—to give up on it simply in the name of "not being off-putting." I believe that we can be welcoming even while wearing robes! At the same time, I consider it not only unreasonable but counterproductive to insist on giving up one's job if one wants to be a priest. One of the reasons I left the monastery where I was practicing is that I very strongly wanted to be a priest, but I wasn't in a position to quit my job, and I certainly wasn't going to force my family to move into a cabin with no running water or heat just because I felt a calling. The people I have ordained continue to live their lives—family, jobs, ordinary responsibilities—and part of being a lay priest is that each of them individually has to figure out how best to merge their vows with an already established life.

This middle path—upholding and continuing the traditions and rituals while adapting them for modern life—is most evident in my decision to deliberately merge my understanding of and training in psychology with my teaching of the dharma. I trained as a psychotherapist and a clinical social worker and saw clients throughout my years of Zen training and teaching. And I have become convinced that practice, especially deep practice, absolutely requires psychological exploration at the same time. Without that psychological exploration, there's a strong possibility that practice can become "spiritual bypassing" (as John Welwood terms it), a way of avoiding or repressing problems in the rest of life by pretending (to self and others) to be enlightened enough not to ever be bothered by anything.[1] Of course, this approach always comes apart under pressure—pretend enlightenment won't help you face a terminal illness, the loss of a loved one, or any other personal tragedy. When you need a grounded practice the most is exactly when practice focused on making you look good fails completely.

There are other reasons I want to merge twenty-first-century Western psychological understanding and the tradition of Zen Buddhism. First, for centuries, a deep commitment to Zen practice was only undertaken by a select few, whose dedication was commonly demonstrated by sitting outside their chosen monastery for days, waiting for the teacher to decide they had proven their commitment. These monks spent most of their lives in monasteries, where every minute of the day, practically every action, was planned and ritualized. This life was hard, but it was simple and focused. For most modern Zen students, life is not only complicated but also fragmented into different contexts—practitioners have to navigate work, relationships, hobbies, a vast array of choices in all aspects of life, and an equally vast array of worries, both individual and social. Practice should be a way to prepare for dealing with all these aspects of life, not a refuge from them. But joining life and practice takes work and guidance. Some few can find a balance on their own, but most people need a mentor, or at least some structure and guidance about what practice can help with, how to best use meditation when in crisis, and where a different kind of help might be more useful. Joining Western psychology to traditional meditation from the start can provide that balance.

Second, American Buddhism has been so secularized that it has lost much of its power. On this topic, yoga is an instructive comparison. When yoga was first brought to the United States by Indian masters like Swami Vivekananda and Paramahansa Yogananda, it was presented as a spiritual practice, of which the physical postures were only a small part. In the 1950s, Richard Hittleman introduced a nonreligious yoga that focused on the physical moves, hoping that this would attract mainstream Americans and motivate them to explore yogic philosophy and meditation. Instead of functioning as a gateway to the other branches of yoga, hatha yoga became separated from them and now—aside from chanting "om" at the start of a class or occasionally practicing breathing exercises—has come to be simply a type of exercise.

The same thing is happening to Buddhism with the current mindfulness craze. Mindfulness is being touted as the answer to everything from PTSD to workers taking too many sick days, but it's been completely abstracted from the philosophical and ethical underpinnings that give it power. It's become a tool to fix a problem rather than a complete shift into a different way of thinking and being. Psychology is a way back to those ethical underpinnings and helps keep Buddhism from following down the path of American yoga.

Of course, psychology itself can be one more way to water down Buddhism. But if psychology is in the service of Buddhism, rather than the other way around, it can help practitioners to overcome the developmental or relational issues that can be a hindrance to practice.

A third reason is that the history of Buddhism in the United States demonstrates that even very advanced practitioners, people who have had deep and sincere awakenings, can lose track of their ethics when faced with the complexity of modern life. The history of Zen in the United States is rife with teachers or advanced meditators becoming addicted to drugs and alcohol, taking sexual advantage of others, or stealing from their centers. Again, I want to point out that for centuries, people who were devoted to practice lived apart from the world and had very few temptations. It is naive and dangerous to expect that a moment of realization means that one will never again make the wrong ethical choice or be tempted to misuse power. I am not suggesting that these teachers did not have genuine awakenings; I truly believe they did. But no matter how powerful the awakening, none of us ever escapes the relative side of life and the complicated and ambiguous choices of everyday life.

Equally troubling is evidence that meditation can, in some

cases, lead to a mental breakdown and even suicide. People suffering from mental health issues may turn to meditation, find some relief, and think this is it: The Answer to All Their Problems. Sometimes these people abandon therapy or medication because they think sitting *zazen* is enough, and they find out too late that meditation is not a panacea. Other times, people who throw themselves into intense practice can lose touch with reality or be unable to integrate a moment of realization with day-to-day living. Concerns about or problems with mindfulness have recently surfaced, and in 2009 a review of mindfulness scholarship looking specifically at reports of negative side effects found that some very serious problems, including dissociation and psychosis, can result from mindfulness.[2] The truth the Buddha offers is radical in its understanding of reality. If that truth is going to be widely available, it should be linked to other tools that help practitioners who lack regular access to a *sangha* and teacher (and even those who do have such access) avoid damaging delusions and misunderstandings.

But even without these rare and serious problems, mindfulness alone is not very useful for truly transforming the root causes of suffering and dissatisfaction. Because secular mindfulness wants to toss the philosophy and ethical structure of Buddhism in the trash, it doesn't actually address the most deep-seated problems of practitioners. We see this problem, this absolute need for spiritual connection and the quest to find it, in all aspects of society. People who get addicted to substances, buy material items constantly, or cycle through relationships are all seeking a larger purpose and a deep sense of connection. They all believe they are not enough in and of themselves, that they need something or someone outside themselves to feel whole, perfect, and complete. My hope is that this book can help people understand that this belief, this story, is just a story.

Finally, as I mentioned above, Buddhists, both long-term, serious practitioners and devotees of secular mindfulness, are prone to spiritual bypassing. As the psychologist and spiritual teacher Robert Augustus Masters notes, humans much prefer to deal with pain by avoidance or repression (often in the form of numbing out) rather than the messy, iterative process of confronting, understanding, and working through that which causes the pain. "Spiritual bypassing fits almost seamlessly into our collective habit of turning away from what is painful, as a kind of higher analgesic with seemingly minimal side effects," writes Masters. "It is a spiritualized strategy not only for avoiding pain but also for legitimizing such avoidance, in ways ranging from the blatantly obvious to the extremely subtle."[3]

It is, unfortunately, all too easy to misunderstand the Buddhist instruction to let go of craving and be present for what is as advocating for an emotionless detachment from the world. This misperception allows people to numb themselves to their suffering rather than penetrate deeply into it as a way to fully understand the nature of suffering itself.

While it is not always successful, I have found that combining psychological exploration with practice helps students understand the need to stick with the practice when strong or upsetting emotions arise and to avoid spiritual bypassing. When I began leading a study group with some of my senior students, at first we worked on koans, and I was lecturing quite a bit. But I quickly realized that I needed to combine sutra and koan study with emotional work to help students see how ancient sutras connected to their current problems and outlooks. Otherwise, the work was all on an intellectual level, and Zen is meant to be a practical, lived engagement with the world. I'm certainly not saying I'm unique in this approach, and neither am I claiming that it works for everyone. But I have found the combination of several tools to be powerful both for advancing practice and for supporting mental health: first, the Abhidharma, which is essentially Buddhist psychology; second, a technique created by Stanley Block called the I-System; and third, the view of reality and the self specifically explored by Zen Buddhism. Drawn from the methods honed in the Soji study groups, this book is designed to teach Buddhist practitioners how to work with the I-System and theories drawn from the Abhidharma in order to uncover and face the things that hold us back in our practices and our lives.

> *The first step to seeing what life requires is for us to understand that to have a self means we are self-centered. Doing zazen we begin to see our patterns, our desires, our needs, and our ego drives, and we begin to realize they are what we call the self. As our practice continues we begin to understand the emptiness and impermanence of these patterns. With this understanding, we can abandon our attachment to them. To do this, we must have patience, persistence, and courage.*

Excerpt from "To Lose the Self Is to Find the Self"
(Dharma talk given at Soji Zen Center, 2009)

MODELS AND REALITY

Before introducing the two systems, the Abhidharma and the I-System, a note of caution. What I am describing are models. These models have utility, but they don't work for everyone, and no one model (whether drawn from Buddhism, psycho-therapy, or elsewhere) can solve everything. Many people want very much to find a model or system that will always work, in all circumstances. While I believe the I-System and the view of reality presented by the Abhidharma are both immensely useful, they are still just models, not reality itself. They are the finger pointing at the moon, not the moon itself.

I also want to note that, while I'm offering a combination of two models, I believe that, in order to have a successful practice, students must dedicate themselves to a particular style of Buddhism or belief system and practice with focus and dedication. One of the unfortunate side effects of our easy access to knowledge is that many people want to dabble. They want to take what they believe are the best parts of several systems and build something that fits them individually. Perhaps that works with some things, but in my years of teaching I have never seen this approach lead to actual change. Instead, people pick and choose aspects of various belief systems that reinforce their existing stories and biases, in a way that inevitably reassures them that what they want to do is what they should do. I hope these materials and exercises are helpful to you, but nothing can replace regular study with a teacher who knows their tradition on a deep, mature level.

Finally, I want to stress that the I-System and the understanding of the self or ego presented in the Abhidharma are tools to clarify and focus the mind. Soon I'll be introducing a tool known as "mind maps." These are a way to externalize and reflect on your bodily and emotional reactions, a way to discover views and attachments you may not even know you had. The mind maps in this book are designed to lead to a state of *positive samadhi*, which is total absorption in some object or activity. Practice in positive samadhi prepares you for zazen, where the goal is to drop off body and mind. For many people, jumping right into zazen is very difficult, and they end up spending a lot of time daydreaming or concentrating on their inner monologue, rather than letting go of thoughts. Introspection can be a useful tool for mental health, but it is not zazen, and much time can be wasted by practitioners who think they are doing zazen when what they are really doing is reinforcing their sense of self by ruminating on problems. But at the same time, the mind maps are not an end in and of themselves. So, with these cautions in mind, here is a brief overview of the two models I will explore in this book.

THE ABHIDHARMA

The Abhidharma is Buddhist psychology in that it is the explanation, based on the Buddha's understanding, of how the mind works—how it perceives and interacts with both itself and the rest of the world. Abhidharmic texts and ideas are complicated and nuanced, and there are many elements. In this book I will be focusing on just a few aspects.

Four classifications from the Abhidharma that I use frequently are the five *skandhas*, the five omnipresent factors, the six realms of existence, and the twelve links of dependent origination. These will be explored more fully in subsequent chapters; for the moment, it is only necessary to understand the basics.

The skandhas are the stuff that make up the ego. Descartes said, "I think, therefore I am." In Buddhism, however, there is no "I," so the tradition suggests, "Thinking, the world is." The skandhas are the elements of how the ego creates and maintains itself.

The five omnipresent factors describe the way we get

hooked into behavior patterns and thus mirror the activity of the skandhas. Whereas the skandhas are about the internal world, the five factors are about how we interact with the external world.

Another way of understanding how we interact with the world is the twelve links of dependent origination. This is the teaching of the chain of causation that leads not only to suffering but rebirth. "Rebirth" here does not mean only literal past and future existences but the continual rebirth of a self—the work that we do many, many times every day to protect the notion that we exist separately from everything that is "not me" and that this difference is both coherent and essential. Recognizing how we move from link to link is an important tool in disrupting the delusions that cause suffering.

Finally, the six realms describe the Buddhist cosmology; there are the three higher realms (the human realm and two god realms—that is, the *devas* and the *asuras*) and three lower realms (the animal, the hungry ghost, and the hell realms). Traditionally, many Buddhists understood these realms as actual places, but they can also be used to describe psychological states we move in and out of every day.

Together, these four psychological models from the Abhidharma help us understand how we create a sense of self, interact with the world through that sense of self, spin out a story line or worldview, and react psychologically to desires and threats, both internal and external.

THE I-SYSTEM

The second model that this book uses is a contemporary psychological concept called the I-System. Created by Stanley H. Block, the I-System is one part of a larger model, known as

Mind-Body Bridging (MBB), for understanding and working through psychological problems. In this book I will refer most often to the I-System because I only use that one section of the Mind-Body Bridging system in my work with my students and also because I continue to use an older model of the system that I find works especially well in conjunction with Zen practice. As described by the Mind-Body Bridging Institute website, MBB is "an internationally recognized clinical and psycho-educational modality, developed by Dr. Stanley H. Block, that optimizes health, wellness, and human performance" by removing the hindrance (the Identity-System) of individual and collective suffering (http://mindbodybridging.com/about-mbb/). With the Identity-System turned off, personal and relational harmony and balance are restored. As with the Abhidharma, I am going to focus on elements of the I-System that I and my students have found especially helpful.

Over the years, I have adapted the I-System model in conjunction with the study of sutras, koan practice, and other Buddhist texts to encourage a combined spiritual and mental well-being and allow practitioners to take their practice off the cushion and into the world. Below is a brief explanation of the elements of the I-System. In the first four chapters of the book, I explore elements of the Abhidharma; in the last four chapters of this book, I combine the Abhidharma and the I-System to help you improve your practice and life. Appendix B also offers a complete glossary of all the I-System terms.

I-SYSTEM BASICS

Our *Identity-System* is the system that creates our sense of self. It insists that we are damaged and that undoing that damage is the key and only way to peace of mind. Out of this sense of damage, we create stories to explain why we are damaged. We thus fall into *requirements* about how we, others, and the world should be. Requirements are "should" or "ought" statements, and they can describe beliefs about the self, such as "I should be able to balance work and family," or beliefs about what others (family, friends, the world in general) owe us, such as "People at work should take me seriously." In each case, the requirement supports the story we tell about what we need to create a sense of balance.

Fixers and *depressors* are attempts to prop up the stories we spin, the first by rushing in to attempt to fix the damage ("If I were more outgoing, I'd be happier—I need to make more friends"), the second by reinforcing the damage so it seems overwhelming ("I'll never make friends"). Fixers are associated with body anxiety—fast breathing, tension, or restlessness. Depressors are associated with body heaviness—pressure, tiredness, or slowed breathing. Both result in mind clutter and body tension, and, most importantly, both reinforce the false belief that the self is damaged. No matter what we try as an attempt to fix the damage, the Identity-System will report back "not enough/not good enough." The only way out of the cycle is to escape from the belief that we are damaged in the first place. This, of course, is intimately connected with the Mahayana (one of the two major divisions of Buddhism and the branch of Buddhism that includes Zen) claim that everything has buddha-nature—everything is whole, perfect, and complete already.

Mind maps are one of the main tools to uncover requirements, fixers, and depressors, and I have adapted this tool to work with Buddhist philosophy. A mind map asks us to write down our responses to a short prompt or question, quickly and without censoring ourselves. By reviewing the answers while sensing for body tension, we can see which ones are most influential; by looking at the pattern of answers, we can see what our story and requirements are.

Bridging is what takes us out of the cycle of the Identity-System and helps us come to our senses. It involves tuning in to background sounds, becoming aware of the pull of gravity, concentrating on the feeling of your feet on the floor or the pen in your hands, or looking closely at the ink as it flows out of the pen. These techniques quiet the cluttered mind and turn off the focus on the self, allowing the mind to rest and clear. You can see from this description that bridging is very close to positive samadhi (total absorption in an object or activity), the only difference being that, while bridging, you are also doing a mind map rather than being completely focused on the external element. Bridging is the first step to the state of total immersion that is samadhi, the state where you no longer experience the self as separate from the rest of the world.

I have found that when the practice of mind maps is combined with meditation and a thoughtful study of the principles of Zen, it is remarkably effective in freeing people from their excuses, their "small mind." This can help people face problems in their practice and their day-to-day lives and thus help Zen students avoid the spiritual bypassing described above.

One common result of spiritual bypassing is that a student who seems very dedicated to the practice suddenly gives it up entirely, either out of frustration or because something new has appeared that the student believes will distract from their fear and suffering better than sitting does. For example, people often give up practice when they start a new relationship because they feel they no longer "need" Buddhism to feel content. Probing deeper into this belief, I have often found that what appears on the surface to be serious study (the student sits multiple times a day and does retreats) is actually still completely centered on appeasing the demands of the ego. Combining the I-System with meditation can also help people avoid the mistake of believing they are meditating, when they are really just strengthening the ego while sitting very still.

AN EXAMPLE OF MIND MAPPING

Consider one of the main ideas of *The Diamond Sutra*—abiding no place, raise the Bodhi mind. This teaching points to the deep truth that freedom from suffering comes with letting go of attachments. But what, precisely, does it mean, in the twenty-first-century United States, to "abide no place"? For the vast majority of Zen students, it does not mean the kind of literal home-leaving practiced by premodern Zen monks, and even less the radical wandering of the earliest Buddhists. How can one "abide no place" when one has a house with a mortgage payment, a job, and a family? Simply offering the phrase as a lofty and abstract goal leads to an unmoored practice that can be easily lost. However, consider what happens when the phrase is transformed into a mind map. The map could feature the actual sentence from the sutra, but maps tend to work better when phrased as a first-person question. So a student might start with the question, "Where do I dwell?" If that still seems a bit abstract, another way to phrase it would be, "What am I attached to?" Here is an example of what a completed map might look like:

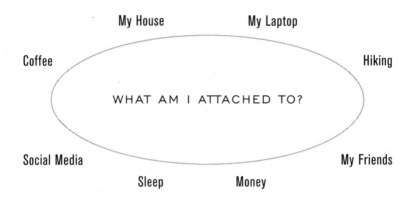

My House   My Laptop

Coffee   Hiking

WHAT AM I ATTACHED TO?

Social Media   My Friends

Sleep   Money

You can do this yourself—take a piece of paper and draw an oval with the words "What am I attached to?" in the center. Then, around the outside of the oval, write down any thoughts that come to mind. Don't censor yourself or try to give the "right" answer. The goal here is to simply note what comes up. For example, one person might write "love, my job, my spouse, my health," while another person might write "the smell of coffee in the morning, starting a new book, checking things off my chores list." Neither is better than the other. What matters is that when students create a mind map around the question "What am I attached to?" or "What makes me who I am?" or simply "Who am I?" then the reality of attachment is unavoidable, and the physical reactions to giving up pieces of identity are out in the open. These reactions—tension in the body or mind—are clues about which of the answers are the most important. The next step is to redo the map with the same question, but this time use the bridging technique of focusing on physical presence instead of the emotions brought up by the thoughts.

The practice looks like this: Get a new blank piece of paper, and draw the oval with the same question inside. As you begin to write your answers (which could be the same or different—don't judge or censor what you find yourself writing), pay attention to the sense of gravity, to your feet on the floor, to the appearance of the ink on the paper, or to any other physical appearance or sensation that's easy for you to tune in to. If you notice yourself slipping into discursive thinking about your answers, simply return your focus to something physical in the present moment.

Hopefully, students will see that this bridging technique does in fact reduce the stress and tension around the stories of identity created by our attachments. This, in turn, can make letting go of attachments while sitting more manageable.

The final step is to move from bridging to zazen. When we bridge, we can recognize that the problem or emotion is not actually part of the present moment. But that recognition can lead to a belief that pushing the feeling away is the answer. When we sit, we become intimate with our feelings; we sink into them. I often tell my students they have to understand their problems or emotions: What size is this emotion? How much does it weigh? What color is it? Then, once we are truly intimate with our feelings, let go even of the intimacy. Drop the emotion and the problem that led to the emotion. Drop off body and mind. Drop everything and just be present. This is the state of samadhi beyond positive samadhi, as you are no longer absorbed in a particular external object or activity but simply in the experience of being alive.

HOW TO USE THIS BOOK

This book is designed to be a practical workbook, something you can use to strengthen your practice and improve your life. The first four chapters provide an in-depth look at the Abhidharma, specifically the four aspects, mentioned above, that I have found particularly helpful for myself and my students. Readers who are unfamiliar with the Abhidharma may want to proceed through those chapters in order, to gain a more thorough understanding of Buddhist psychology. The next three chapters of the book offer guided instructions for engaging with the Abhidharma using mind maps. Readers who are eager to start delving into mind mapping or who are strongly engaged by one of the Abhidharma chapters may wish to skip back and forth between these two sections. Chapter 1, "The Skandhas," is paired with the mind maps in chapter 5; chapters 2 and 3, which cover the omnipresent factors and dependent origination, are linked to chapter 6; and chapter 4, on the six realms, is connected to chapter 7. Chapter 8 includes maps that I have designed specifically around meditation practice, and Chapter 9 connects some of the major sutras to mind maps. Although there are copies of the maps in the book, I recommend drawing your own ovals on separate paper; that way you can revisit the maps over and over and see the prompt with fresh eyes.

I recommend doing a mind map every day for at least the first month or two, in order to become familiar with the process and to see how your answers change as you do bridging maps. It's not necessary to do maps right before sitting or to do a map every time you sit; decide what works best for you. It's also up to you whether you stick to doing one prompt or do different prompts. I certainly recommend revisiting a prompt regularly and keeping your past maps (I use a three-ring binder), so you can compare answers, body tension, and mind clutter. But it's best to do a map that directly addresses what is happening in your life at that moment and keep doing the map as long as the issue is present. If there's no pressing concern or question, you can return to an earlier map and redo it. And of course, you can do more than one map a day!

Before we delve further into exploring the Abhidharma and the I-System, it is important to understand that they do not replace sitting meditation. Without a regular sitting practice, these exercises will be only a little helpful. The ancient masters used to say that a picture of a rice cake won't satisfy hunger; today we might say that reading a cookbook won't get dinner made. Please don't think that mind maps can replace sitting! But, for the reasons described above, I have come to believe that today sitting itself is no longer enough. For too many people, "Buddhism" has become "mindfulness," and meditation has become nothing more than a way to calm down or bliss out. This all comes out of small mind—we're trying to fix the problem with the same mind that caused the problem! It all goes back to fear and especially the fear of nonexisting. So we secularize Buddhism (perhaps relying on guided meditations from the internet or mindfulness apps) in ways that support our stories rather than challenging them. In my view, we look at our stories to see where we're stuck, but then we should take a further step to see that the story is just a story, a fabrication. It's all dualistic; improving your story is still about reinforcing the dualism rather than transcending it. In the West we need interventions, such as mind mapping, that comprise a kind of cultural support for "leaving home" and practicing intently, as well as providing structures for individuals, so they don't end up simplifying zazen into "fifteen minutes of free time."

When I first started practicing, I had a belief that a spiritual awakening would address and reduce psychological and developmental issues. This didn't prove true for me or, as far as I can tell, anyone else—one can have incredible transcendental experiences but still be hampered by psychological and developmental issues. The various scandals that have plagued leaders of Buddhist centers are proof of that. One can be enlightened and still do messed-up things, treat people badly, struggle with addiction, and so forth. This is because we can never exist purely in the realm of the absolute—being enlightened doesn't mean spending the rest of your life floating on a lotus flower in a beam of light. In fact, the opposite is true, as the "Ten Ox-Herding Pictures" make clear. These ten pictures illustrate the search for enlightenment, here pictured as an ox. After finding, taming, and then transcending the ox, the journey seems to be complete by the ninth picture, but there is a tenth—returning to the world. The tenth picture shows the monk in a marketplace, doing all the ordinary things of life, often interacting with another person for the first time in the series. In the end, enlightenment means nothing if we have to cut ourselves off from the world to maintain it.

The mind maps, when combined with aspects of the Abhidharma, allow us to both pinpoint the stories we tell ourselves and see how we continue to be tangled in the beliefs of those stories. However, a regular, dedicated practice of zazen is necessary to solidify the changes that come from seeing our stories as stories, and internalizing the precepts (the ethical underpinning of Buddhism) allows us to practice off the cushion, when we're in the busy world. Precepts, zazen, Buddhist psychology, and mind maps all address different aspects of life and point out how we are driven by dualistic views. Mind maps and the exercises here aren't about changing Buddhism; rather, they're about providing another path to the same truths.

A NOTE ON DHARMA TALKS

I have never wanted to do a collection of my dharma talks. Talks gain much of their power from the immediate experience, the intimacy of teacher and students in the same room. Even listening to a recorded talk is a pale echo of hearing a talk live, seeing the speaker, sitting among other practitioners. Reading a transcript of a talk means even more is lost. But my students suggested that excerpts from talks would be a valuable addition to the book, so you will find in each chapter a few paragraphs from one or two talks I have given. Sometimes the connection between the chapter's focus and the talk will be obvious, sometimes less so, but either way I hope the excerpts provide another way to think about the ideas presented through the lenses of the Abhidharma and the I-System.

When we begin to explore through sitting, we inevitably encounter the wild and uncontrollable aspects of our habitual mind. But with some guidance and skillful practice, we begin to recognize that the mind has an undercurrent of clarity and luminosity. To awaken this innate clarity is to awaken to our buddha-nature. We can enter into a state free of much of the psychological distress that comes from our belief that we are this limited, separate self.

This freedom can be understood as the healing that arises

from the depth of our being when we get even a glimpse of our true nature—which is as part of the greater whole of the One Body. We must constantly remind ourselves that the goal is not something outside of us; it is our own true nature, the nature we can easily lose sight of in our complicated, high-pressure, and often destructively materialistic culture.

"A VISION OF WHOLENESS," 2010

1

THE SKANDHAS

THE ABHIDHARMA IS an early and very detailed set of writings that can be described as Buddhist psychology and that, in a sense, underlies all subsequent Buddhist teachings. Yet it is not often studied in American Buddhism, in part because the focus of our practice has been sitting and also because it is a very dense, detailed, and complicated work. The Abhidharma is actually more of a category of Buddhist literature than a single text—it exists in different complete and partial versions in several Asian languages. The translation I use is over four hundred pages long, and I will only be talking about a few elements that relate directly to the I-System and that aid in deepening practice. (For those who are interested in learning more about the Abhidharma, there is a good online version available at the BuddhaNet website: http://www.bud dhanet.net/pdf_file/abhidharma.pdf.)

What is most important to remember about the Abhidharma is that it describes existence as a process. *Everything* is a process—there is nothing (no external thing and no internal self or soul) that is fixed and unchanging. The Abhidharma explores in depth the Buddha's teachings of interdependence and impermanence—all the ways one thing contributes to and leads to another. It also explores how we are constantly recreating ourselves—literally, our sense of self—out of patterns of reactions to physical and mental stimuli.

BUDDHISM AND CONSCIOUSNESS

Before we delve into our first psychological model from the Abhidharma, the skandhas, it is important to understand how Buddhism views consciousness. Although Western philosophy and science do recognize the complexity of truly knowing what consciousness is and how it functions, in general, consciousness today is understood as singular—"consciousness" is awareness of the external world or of self. Instead of this straightforward view of consciousness, which lumps the totality of all kinds of awareness into one "consciousness," Buddhism describes nine different levels of consciousness. The first six levels are sense consciousnesses—seeing, hearing, tasting, smelling, touching, and thinking. (In Buddhism, thoughts are considered a sense because just like the eyes process visual impressions, the mind processes mental impressions.) So seeing an object is one kind of awareness, while smelling it or touching it would be another kind of awareness.

One thing this approach does is shift focus from higher-level thinking to sentience. When Zen students chant the "Four Great Bodhisattva Vows," they vow to save all "sentient beings," including but not limited to all humans. If a being can see, taste, hear, smell, or feel, Buddhism recognizes it as sentient and worthy of respect and compassion. The other result of this approach is to recognize all the different ways we interact with the world. We know, of course, that smelling a rose is a different experience than seeing it, but considering these different experiences of consciousness is an important step toward understanding how we generate reactions to both the external world and to our mental impressions.

The seventh level of consciousness is that of ego. This is the level of self-awareness, of a discrete sense of self, but it's important to understand that this level is a delusion. If nothing is permanent and separate from the rest of existence, then the idea that there is an ego, a self, a "you" that is coherent and unchanging is simply not true. Ego consciousness is always active, evaluating and judging what it likes and does not like according to how things support or interfere with its sense of itself. This is where suffering arises—the ego, in its struggle to create a sense of coherent stability out of what is really a stream of constant change, insists that there is a clear distinction between "self" and "not-self" and evaluates everything based on the need to maintain that belief.

This leads to suffering in two ways. First, supporting the belief that the self is permanent and unchanging is exhausting because it requires constantly evaluating whatever arises to see if it threatens this delusion. The mind can never rest because it is constantly scanning to see if there is a challenge to its existence as a coherent and stable whole. Second, splitting the world into "self" and "not-self" automatically leads to discrimination—thoughts such as "I like this and want to keep it" and "I don't like that and want to get rid of it" must arise because that is how the self establishes its existence. We can never have everything we think we want, and we can never get rid of everything we think we don't want. Thus, we find ourselves in a condition in which we're inevitably unsatisfied with our existence, even as we buy wholeheartedly into the belief that our existence is the most important truth in the entire world.

The eighth level of consciousness is called the "store-house" (in Sanskrit *alaya*). In this level all past experiences are stored, as well as the seeds of both delusion and enlightenment. In one way, the eighth level is similar to the unconscious, in that most people cannot access it directly, yet it has a profound influence on our actions and beliefs. If you find yourself trapped in a pattern of behavior—grabbing donuts right after declaring a diet, for example, or becoming enraged when a partner gets *that tone of voice*, despite promising yourself not to overreact—you are experiencing the power of the storehouse consciousness. Another way to think about this is to think about the modern understanding of genetics. Two people might smoke the same number of cigarettes, but only one develops lung cancer because of genetic differences. Neither karma nor genes mean a person is fated to a certain path, but they do make that path more likely, especially if people are not conscious of their influences.

The ninth level is that of pure consciousness, our original and universal consciousness that is the absolute side of reality. Here there is no karmic activity and no sense of self and other. Some Buddhist sects teach that this level can be accessed by chanting or very deep meditation, while other sects believe it is reached only during an awakening experience or that it is not consciously accessed at all. What is important here is to understand that Buddhism considers there to be a level of awareness, of consciousness, beyond individual awareness.

Both Buddhism and the I-System start from the premise that we are innately perfect and then explore why we think the exact opposite. In subsequent chapters, I will be referring to these levels of consciousness and asking you to explore how they create a sense of self, a place in the world, and an impression that we are not whole, perfect, and complete.

Ego provides the standpoint from which we see the world around us, and consciousness is what we experience by asking, "What is that?" and replying, "It's such-and-such." Thus, ego congeals life into facts, which are fixed and which must be clung to. Everything perceived and experienced is seen from the standpoint of the self and related to the self— and becomes the antiself.

Things are "real" only to the extent that they are rooted in this objective reality, which is itself pinned down in concepts. This means that nothing is real unless it has been or can be integrated within a conceptual system. When we identify with the ego, we see the reality presented to us by the ego as the whole of reality and dismiss as unreal anything that has not been made, or cannot be made, to fit in with it. In the same way, the only thing that makes us real is having a definite standpoint and sticking to it.

We think that there is nothing outside the ego, and we assume that the whole of reality and ourselves will go if we drop ego—that if the ego ceases to be, meaningful reality disappears with it. Zen says that far from nothing being left behind when the ego is dropped, our true nature is released, and true reality dawns.

"OBJECTIVE CONSCIOUSNESS," 2009

THE SKANDHAS

Now let's turn to the skandhas and elaborate on the brief description I gave in the introduction. *Skandha* literally means "heap" or "aggregate," and it is also sometimes translated as "collection." There are five skandhas, and together they make up the internal sense of self—the ego, if you will. The first skandha is form (*rupa*), and it includes all the physical aspects of a person. It is often easiest to see impermanence in form—we all get sick, grow old, and die. The physical changes we go through as we age can be shocking sometimes because mentally we don't feel like we've changed, but the person in the mirror looks very different. On the other hand, it can be hard to see the delusive division of self and other in terms of form—the body seems to have clear boundaries. But we constantly breathe in air. We consume a variety of food and drink, and we excrete waste. We see things because light enters our retinas. Even smells are literally atoms of other forms entering our noses and becoming part of us. With a little thought, we can see that the supposedly clear boundaries between the body and the rest of the world are quite fluid. From a Buddhist perspective, nothing is separate because everything is interdependent.

The other four skandhas are all mental aspects and describe the way we create consciousness. The second skandha is feeling (*vedana*), also translated as "sensation." This is the immediate, visceral reaction someone has to a thing, an experience, or a thought. These reactions broadly fall into three categories: pleasant, unpleasant, and neutral. We all tend to move toward what we find pleasant, move away from what we find unpleasant, and ignore what we find neutral.

The third skandha is perception (*samjna*), which can also be translated as "conception." This is the moment immediately following feeling, when the mind reaches for an association, definition, or understanding. It's this level that starts the process of clinging, of being hooked into a reaction based on past responses. The human brain very much likes patterns—any information that can be put into a preexisting category will be put into one. This is not bad—if our brains hadn't evolved as pattern-recognition machines, we never would have been able to create incredibly complex patterns like art and smartphones. But all sorts of snap judgments and prejudices arise from this tendency. In the split second of the third skandha, ego consciousness asserts that perception *is* reality. To give up the certainty of one's perceptions is to give up the comforting sense of solidity and structure.

The fourth skandha (*samskara*) is sometimes called mental formation or conceptualization, but I prefer the term "discrimination," not only because it is less abstract than the other two but because of the connotations it carries. This is the moment the mind categorizes, interprets, and rationalizes a perception, gives it weight. It is here that the idea of a self is established as a basis for making choices. This is also the level of doing or action—not necessarily physical action but the action of pattern. Once the third level has established which pattern this particular moment fits into, the brain busily reinforces that pattern, noticing only what will support the identification and seeing the pattern rather than what is actually occurring. This level also carries the implication of repetition and proliferation. The more the pattern is accepted as reality, the more it is repeated and the more ingrained it becomes.

The fifth and final skandha (*vijana*) is confusingly translated as "consciousness," but this does not mean that there has been no consciousness until this moment. Consciousness is found in all the skandhas—we can't relate to form if we don't have consciousness. The fifth level is what pulls together the preceding levels, the outcome of the skandha process. Another translation is "awareness," and perhaps this is clearer since it gets at what is essential about this skandha: the awareness is not of other things but of self. Just as the seventh level of consciousness is the ego level, the fifth skandha is the moment when the mind seeks confirmation of the self through the interaction with things that are "not-self." In other words, the mind always places "you" (the ego's created sense of unity) at the center of your life story and constructs everything you encounter and every thought you have as an indication of your separate existence. We do this completely unconsciously most of the time, to the point where this tendency can be a joke: "Of course it's raining; I forgot my umbrella." The ridiculousness of thinking the entire weather system is dictated by your forgetting your umbrella is clear. But it's a short step from that to a sports fan's belief that their team wins, in part, because they wear their lucky shirt, and another short step to thinking a stranger looking in our direction must be paying attention to and thinking about us, or that if a partner is upset, they must be upset about something we did.

The example I use with students to explain the skandhas is to clap my hands. The first level is awareness without definition, just an experience of the sound. The second level, in the student's mind, is to hear the sound and have a reaction to it (to experience the sound as pleasant, unpleasant, or neutral). The third level, which follows so closely that people often can't see the distinction between the sensation and the perception, is to think, "He clapped his hands." The fourth level is to categorize that perception and fit it into a pattern, to realize, "He clapped his hands to make a point." The fifth level is to relate this point, this pattern, to the self: "I remember when so-and-so clapped her hands," or, "I know what point he's trying to make by clapping his hands." In just a second or two, the student moves from the straightforward awareness of an experience to a complex and intellectual understanding of what the experience "means," and that meaning reinforces the student's sense of self.

Cycling through the skandhas happens hundreds of times a day. There's nothing inherently wrong or bad about that cycle as long as we understand that it is our minds, our egos, that are building complex meanings into things and events, not that the things and events themselves inherently carry those meanings. The fact that we are often right about what the patterns mean should not delude us into thinking the patterns are reality—that's storytelling. For example, imagine you are at work and your boss snaps at you. Being snapped at is unpleasant, no doubt. But the next moment, when your ego leaps to create a self-centered understanding of the experience, unless you have the awareness that that understanding is a construct, you have left reality behind. Your thought that they snapped at you because they're angry with your work is just that—a thought—*even if* they snapped at you because they're angry with your work. Just because the reality of the situation catches up to and matches your ego's storytelling doesn't mean the story is any less a story.

You may be tempted to think, "This has nothing to do with me; they probably just got caught in bad traffic or didn't get enough sleep." But this is replacing one story (it's all about me) with another story (it's all about them). From the I-System perspective, this is a fixer, a way to offset uncomfortable feelings by creating a story that explains or excuses those feelings. It's an easy trap to fall into and in fact is often recommended as a way to deal with anxiety or anger, but the truth of the matter is that relocating the cause of the emotion still doesn't deal with your feelings of anger or get at the core belief of the I-System, that you believe you're inherently damaged. Understanding how the skandhas create ego consciousness begins to help us see to the core of this fundamental issue.

Breaking down all the skandhas to explain them makes them sound static, so I want to make clear that the skandhas are a process and specifically a process of avoidance. They are stages in a dynamic whereby the self is continually recreated and maintained. The focus of the mind is not on fully engaging with the world but on avoiding anything that might disrupt the sense of self. The skandhas are an internal or inward-facing response to the impermanence of reality and to the truth that we are not actually fixed, continuous, and separate from the rest of the world.

In the next chapter, we will discuss the omnipresent factors, which are an outward-facing response to those same realities. Before turning to that Buddhist model, however, I would like to take a moment to compare the skandhas and the I-System.

THE SKANDHAS AND THE I-SYSTEM

The Identity-System is similar to the process of ego creation described by the skandhas in that the Identity-System is the belief that we are damaged, incomplete, and not good enough. Here and in many subsequent cases I am using "I-System" to refer not to the overall model but specifically the internal monologue and mind clutter we all experience. This constant mental chatter is us watching and evaluating ourselves, and this "identity-system" always finds fault with us. The skandhas create a sense of self, of consciousness, and when they do so outside of our awareness, they push the mind toward obsession with maintaining that sense of self. Everything is processed through this perceived need, and anything seen as a threat to the sense of a stable self creates mind clutter and body tension. While the I-System model is not as concerned with distinguishing the steps by which a belief is created, both the I-System and the skandhas demonstrate how much of our mental energy is spent on supporting and defending beliefs about ourselves and our view of reality.

Case 29 of the Gateless Gate: *A temple flag was flapping in the wind. Two monks were arguing: one said the flag was moving; the other said the wind was moving. The Sixth Patriarch said, "It is neither the wind nor the flag that moves; it is your mind."*

These two monks were actually engaging in recreating and reinforcing their concept of self. They set up a split between self and nonself. In Buddhism, this is known as the first skandha. The split between self and not-self that emerges in the first skandha also takes place within the self. We like the good, adequate, competent self we hope we are and dislike the bad, inadequate, unlovable, deficient, and unworthy self we fear that we may be.

When I swing my arms, you can see my sleeves moving. It's just this: not minds, not the body, not the past, not the future, not even the present, but just this. It is not me, not others, not all sentient beings. Just this! But it is not even this, that, or it. We are as we are and nothing else. And even when we say, "We are as we are," we are far away from the truth.

"Neither the Wind nor the Flag," 2013

SUMMARY OF THE SKANDHAS

Form (rupa)—all the physical aspects that make up a thing (for a person, the body).
A person's hands.

Sensation (vedana)—the moment of contact with something.
The sound of hands clapping.

Perception (samjna)—the instant response to the thing and the patterns of response that follow immediately.
"He clapped his hands." "I don't like that noise."

Discrimination (samskara)—labeling the response, the mental action, in the sense of fitting the contact into a pattern.
"He clapped his hands to make a point." "Clapping means approval."

Awareness (vijnana)—the creation of consciousness, centering the self and relating to the thing in terms of how it threatens or reinforces the self.
"I understand what point he's trying to make by clapping his hands."

2

THE OMNIPRESENT
FACTORS

THE SKANDHAS ARE a way of understanding the internal
world, how the self creates and defines its existence in terms
of desire, pattern, and ego. The five omnipresent factors
(also called the common factors) mirror the skandhas but
explore the way the self relates to the rest of the world. In the
Abhidharma, the omnipresent factors are defined as the elements that make up the unenlightened state, a description
of the stages the ordinary, conditional mind cycles through
when faced with things or actions of the outside world. The
factors are often easier for people to grasp than the skandhas
because we are all much more familiar with desire for or aver-
sion to something "out in the world" while being less aware
of the processes happening inside our minds in relation to
the creation of self. You'll notice as you read about the five
factors that many of the terms are the same as the skandhas,
and when they are not actually the same, they are nonethe-
less obviously connected. This is a key point—the skandhas
and the omnipresent factors work together to create a sense
of self and other and to locate happiness in getting everything that is other into the desired state. Of course, we can
never attain even a moment when everything in the world is

exactly as we want it, and thus happiness cannot be found outside ourselves. It doesn't stop us from trying!

The first of the omnipresent factors is often labeled "invested contact," although a simpler translation is "grasping at experience." The Sanskrit term is *sparsha*. This factor covers every moment when we grasp or cling to an experience or designate a thing as necessary for our happiness. It's important to understand that there is a difference between desire and clinging to desire. One of the most common mistakes people make about Buddhism is to think that its goal is to give up all desire, to become completely detached from everything. Aside from the fact that this is impossible, it is simply not the goal of Zen. In fact, one of the three essentials for awakening in Zen (aside from great faith and great doubt) is great determination. We cannot awaken to our true nature without a great deal of determination and effort, and determination can only arise from a desire for awakening. What the first factor describes is not simple desire but grasping after an experience and seeing it as essential to happiness, which really means essential to the ego's view of itself as stable, fixed, and permanent.

To give a simple example of the difference between desire and clinging, imagine you are going out to your favorite restaurant, a place you love to eat. You are looking forward to eating the special dish you always get. But when you arrive, you discover the owners are on vacation and the restaurant is closed. If your day is ruined, you are in the grip of invested contact—you have willfully placed your sense of happiness in an external experience, and since everything is impermanent, you are sure to be disappointed at some point. If, however, you can let go of the desire to have that dish and instead enjoy yourself at another restaurant eating something else entirely, you are not grasping. To dig into the clinging reaction a bit more: isn't it the case that you were clinging to that special dish because it helps define your sense of self by creating pattern, routine, a sense of stability? "I am the person who eats this dish at this restaurant" is a kind of stability, but so is "I am an adventurous person who always tries a new dish." Even if the pattern is change, it's still a pattern that helps us define the self as stable.

The second factor, like the second skandha, is *vedana*, here translated as the "attractive or aversive reaction to a thing" instead of just the internal feeling. Every experience has a feeling tone, and too often we think that tone is inherent in the experience rather than arising from us. This is manifestly untrue. Two people ride the same roller coaster: one finds the experience exhilarating, while the other is terrified. Two people eat the same spicy dish: one loves the level of heat, while the other feels sick. Again, the important thing here is not to deny the reaction, to feel bad or "unenlightened" for having a certain reaction. What matters is recognizing that the reaction arises within us and is not an external force over which we have no control.

Of course, don't make the opposite mistake of thinking we have perfect control over our reactions! That's just as much of a story told by the ego as believing everything is beyond our control. People often twist themselves into knots by believing that they should be in control at all times and that they are responsible for everything that happens to them. This is another misunderstanding of Buddhism—that being enlightened means having perfect control over your emotions and never being bothered by anything. I've met people I believe to be deeply enlightened, and I can assure you they all still get pissed off, sad, and elated. The idea that we can completely control everything is another manifestation of the story that our ego is separate from the rest of reality. I'm afraid you'll have to let go of that belief along with everything else.

The third factor might be considered a combination of the third and fourth skandhas, perception and discrimination. This factor is known as entrancement (*samjna*), getting hooked into patterns. At first glance it seems like people get hooked into patterns they think are positive, that feel rewarding or soothing. In fact, being hooked into *any* pattern is much more important than whether that pattern is positive or negative because it's the pattern itself that creates the illusion of stability and security (both in the world and in the sense of self). It's amazingly common for people to self-sabotage in order to protect the belief that their pattern is "true." Someone who believes he is unlovable will pick a fight with a new partner rather than risk losing that identity. Someone who thinks of herself as "being fat" will sabotage one diet after another in order to maintain a physical reality that matches her mental picture. I see this all the time in Zen practice: People will come to the practice because they are suffering deeply, and at first, they will sit and sit and start to feel better. But as soon as their practice moves past a superficial sense of calm, as soon as it forces them to confront the inherent unreality of their self, they abandon Buddhism. Sometimes they'll even admit they're afraid of what comes up, although more often they just disappear.

Sometimes students who leave tell me they need a less ritual-heavy version of Buddhism; the way some students will suddenly believe that a particular type of Buddhism is not what they want and that they need to make a change is actually an example of the fourth factor: self-motivated intentionality (*chetana*).

Self-motivated intentionality—what does that even mean? It's the way we make everything about us—our self and our ego. Just as the fifth skandha is about centering the ego, this fourth factor is about continually reinforcing the sense of self by making reality all about us. Another way of translating this factor would be as "will" or "volition." Herbert Guenther, one of the early European scholars of Buddhist philosophy, writes, "It is a mental event that arouses and urges the mind with its corresponding events on towards an object."[4] In other words, it is the step when, while craving something (mentally or physically), we are moved to action toward attaining or rejecting the thing. A student who feels shaky after confronting the essential unreality of the ego will find that a dharma talk I give to the whole sangha is a pointed insult to them, or advice I give about their practice is an attack. Understanding the talk or advice as "all about me" gives one an excuse to leave practice without admitting that one is unnerved by the truths that have come up. This is not to say that I'm a perfect teacher! I'm not at all suggesting that no one is ever deliberately rude, offensive, or a bully. But even when someone is overtly and deliberately insulting you, your reaction can still be based in the factor of self-motivated intentionality, making the interaction all about you and only you.

The fifth and final factor is called invested attention (*manskara*). This is the selective view of the world we all engage in, based on our self-interest and attachment to our patterns. This is a step beyond beliefs about the self—it is filtering information in order to reinforce the beliefs we already have. The fifth factor applies to everything from the sense that our partner "always" does that thing we hate to automatically trusting what our political party says (and automatically disbelieving everything the other side says). In psychology, this is known as confirmation bias and—specifically in terms of self-image—self-verification. Studies have shown that people don't remember feedback that conflicts with their self-image as well as they do feedback that reinforces that sense of self.[5] An even more extreme example is that people who are shown proof that a core belief they have is based on incorrect information actually hold that belief *more* strongly than before.[6] This is because the goal of the self is to preserve the sense of permanence and stability. When threatened with a sense of instability, the ego will double down and reinterpret, reject, or simply ignore any information that might create any further sense of destabilization. This would be bad enough if we all had healthy egos that interpreted reality through a lens of openness and positive engagement, but most of us, to greater or lesser degrees, have unhealthy egos that perceive the world through a lens of fear or anger (or both).

If you recall that the eighth level of consciousness is the storehouse, where the seeds of our behavior are formed, you'll see the connection between the eighth consciousness and the fifth omnipresent factor, invested attention. Both models hold that we do not engage with the patterns consciously. Instead, they are subconscious—and all the more powerful because of it.

An example of the omnipresent factors at work came early in my teaching career. At first my vision was to teach Iaido, the Japanese art of drawing and cutting with a sword. I thought I would incorporate Zen into Iaido, to ground the physical practice in the spiritual. I found that martial artists were gung ho at first about Zen, but they either didn't stick with it or didn't appreciate the complexity of Zen. In fact, one weekend I gave a workshop at the Village Zendo, and when I returned the following weekend, I found that a guy who had several black belts had taken over and was trying to teach Zen! This was an example of the factors at work: he was so hooked into the pattern of being an authority that he honestly believed a single workshop was all he needed to be a Zen teacher. Here the fourth and fifth factors are especially powerful. Self-motivated intentionality made it important that he be perceived as "the expert" in everything; this was how he maintained a sense of consistent self in relation to the rest of the world. And the fifth factor, invested attention, automatically filtered the workshop information so that he remembered and valued all the parts of Zen that were similar to what he knew about martial arts and ignored and devalued those parts that were significantly different.

Part of the work of both the I-System and zazen is to make us aware of these unconscious patterns. But just becoming aware is not enough—bringing patterns to the surface of our mind and examining them is the work of therapy, but in Buddhism this is only viewed as a preliminary step. The ultimate goal is to develop the skill to notice when you have started to evaluate things in a way that reinforces the self and to withdraw energy from that evaluation or stop altogether. But that, as I said in the first chapter, is very hard to do, especially by oneself. And in the modern world, where we are all familiar with psychological terms, it's especially easy to fall into a focus on just feeling better. So first we do a mind map so that we can see the source of our distress. Then we move to bridging in order to separate our feelings from the present moment. But that is not the final step—that comes in zazen, when thoughts come up and we drop them and eventually drop our sense of self. These are the psychological and the transcendent levels of existence, and they work wonderfully together.

Another connection to understand is how all of this—the seventh and eighth levels of consciousness, the skandhas, and now the omnipresent factors—is an articulation of the second noble truth, the truth that suffering exists because of clinging. We often think of the second noble truth as only referring to clinging to a desire for things, but in reality, it is about clinging to the belief in the separate and unchanging self as well as the things that this self has invested in. By understanding all the ways that the mind continually creates this self, we can begin to let go of the delusion that the separate and unchanging "I" exists. This, in turn, helps us let go of the clinging that hadn't even seemed like clinging before.

The hedonist and the Zen teacher are both stuck with the fact of the here and now. But the Zen teacher gives life to all events and enters them completely and without reservation. On the other hand, the hedonist avoids certain events and strives to manage his or her life in such a way as to only enter fully those situations that have been judged (that is, prejudged) as worthwhile.

The everyday life of the Zen master consists of merely eating rice and drinking tea. In other words, an enlightened person is one who has learned not to kill ordinary acts such as eating plain rice or drinking plain tea. What I mean by this is that we should not kill our ordinary everyday lives. We can kill them by living them in a semistupor, in unawareness, mechanically, stupidly, as if we were drugged. Second, we can kill our life by discriminating, devaluing, and demeaning, which occurs when we prefer one situation or thing over another because we believe it is more valuable. If you have tea but want and yearn for wine, you are killing the experience of drinking the tea.

"SHINZAN QUESTIONS THE NATURE OF LIFE," 2015

THE RARE FACTORS

Finally, I want to briefly talk about the rare factors, which are the omnipresent factors transformed by enlightenment. These are what we are working toward with the I-System and sitting. The first factor, invested contact, is transformed into mindfulness (*smriti*), a peaceful presence in the moment. This is what we achieve partially through bridging (which we'll explore more thoroughly and experientially beginning in chapter 6) and mainly through zazen. The second factor, attractive or aversive reaction, is transformed into composure (*samadhi*), the ability to remain calm and centered rather than reactive. You may recognize the word *samadhi* from the earlier mention of "positive samadhi." In meditation, positive samadhi involves counting the breaths or working on a koan. The normal, logical, sequential activities of consciousness are arrested while the mind is completely focused on whatever it is concentrating on. Absolute samadhi (often just called samadhi) is the condition of total stillness—body and mind dropped off, no thought. The mind is empty, yet one is in a state of extreme wakefulness. This is a state of pure existence.

The third factor, getting hooked into patterns, is transformed into a deep knowing of reality, also called transcendental wisdom (*prajna*). The Buddhist idea of wisdom is different than the usual Western definition, where it is linked to soundness of judgment and wide experience. Prajna is not about knowing a great deal of information but about meeting the present moment from a place, as Bernie Glassman, the first dharma successor of Taizan Maezumi and founder of the Zen Peacemakers, says of *not* knowing, not reacting from our preconceived ideas. When we are composed and aware of reality rather than being trapped by our ego, we can respond to situations authentically and from a place of compassion.

This, in turn, allows us to transform the fourth factor, self-motivated intentionality, into aspiration, the vow mind (*chanda*). Zen practitioners take the "Four Great Bodhisattva Vows," the first of which is a vow to save every sentient being. To decenter the self and what the self wants and replace it with vow mind is to be a bodhisattva, an enlightened being.

Finally, invested attention is transformed into reverent appreciation (*adhimoksha*) so that, instead of selectively engaging only with what reinforces our sense of self, we respond out of our natural compassion and gratitude for what is.

The rare factors are aptly named; it is not easy to transform our usual patterns and reactions into the enlightened response of a bodhisattva. This is the work of a lifetime, and we never completely achieve this state of being, any more than we have a moment of awakening and never feel angry or greedy again. While I certainly encourage you to keep the rare factors in mind, I urge you not to set them up as goals or markers of whether your practice is correct or advancing. Instead, I'd suggest you just be aware of the moments when you are operating from the place of one or more rare factors and remind yourself that such states of mind are possible.

THE FACTORS AND THE I-SYSTEM

Just like the omnipresent factors, the I-System also focuses on the way humans continually and unconsciously seek happiness and completion from sources outside of the self. In the I-System, the attractive reactions are known as fixers, and the aversive reactions are known as depressors. These are the things that keep the Identity-System active. On a psychological level, mind maps allow us to pinpoint the things we think we need to have or need to get rid of and thus help make clear to the conscious mind that this thinking is not in line with reality. Actually writing down the idea that a new car, a new job, dating successfully, or losing ten pounds would in some way result in lasting happiness reveals the absurdity of that idea. Mapping those beliefs onto the factors and seeing how they spiral from a specific desire to a complete worldview and then sitting quietly in zazen with the truth of this realization can permanently change the way you relate to the claims your ego continually presents as absolutely necessary. And over time, being aware of and calmly present with these reactions instead of immediately moving to fix things can result in the transmutation of the common factors into the rare factors. In the psychological terms of the I-System, this process can result in quieting the Identity-System and allowing the Executive Function to operate unimpeded.

SUMMARY OF THE OMNIPRESENT FACTORS

Sparsha—invested contact, grasping at experience.

Vedana—attractive or aversive reaction.

Samjna—entrancement, getting hooked into our patterns of association.

Chetana—self-motivated intentionality.

Manskara—invested attention, selective viewing motivated by self-interest.

3

THE TWELVE LINKS OF DEPENDENT ORIGINATION

DEPENDENT ORIGINATION AND EMPTINESS

Dependent origination is a core teaching of the Buddha; in fact, some accounts hold that it was the realization of dependent origination as the fundamental truth of the universe that led to Shakyamuni's awakening. In its most compact or elemental form, this is the realization that everything is related to and dependent on everything else—there is nothing in existence that is apart from the rest. So, clearly, this teaching is very important to Buddhism, to understanding the Abhidharma, and to working with the I-System successfully.

Before moving on to talk about the twelve links, which is the expanded, step-by-step understanding of the truth of dependent origination, I would like to say a few words about emptiness. Perhaps no other key Buddhist term (except perhaps "desire") is more easily misunderstood, because the Buddhist definition of "emptiness" is almost exactly opposite from the common Western definition. In the West, "empty" signifies a lack or void, the absence of something. If we say a glass is empty, we mean there is no liquid in it (although of course the glass is full of air!). In Buddhism, however, emptiness is most emphatically *not* a void or lack. It is the term used to recognize that nothing has an intrinsic existence or nature but only exists because of its interdependent connection to all other things. In other words, that glass is "empty" because it cannot exist apart and separate from the rest of the world.

There are two ways to conceptualize this. A way that squares easily with our modern worldview is to remember that science teaches us that everything is made up of the same particles, so there really is no significant difference between you and this book. Both are just particular, temporary arrangements of atoms. A second way, drawn from Buddhism, is to think deeply about how dependent everything is on everything else and how nothing really disappears completely; it just changes form. A seed becomes a tree, which bears fruit. The fruit is eaten and becomes part of the bird that eats it. The bird later dies. The dead body is absorbed by the earth and turned into the raw material for another seed to grow into another tree. Of course, the goal of Zen is not to understand emptiness conceptually but to experience the truth of it in a personal and embodied way.

The strongest, most pernicious view held by human beings is that there is a permanent, immutable, and independent self. Anxiety arises because of a deep awareness that in fact nothing is permanent, immutable, or independent. Humans create notions such as the self, the psyche, and the soul to assuage the anxiety caused by this truth. In doing so, we create more anxiety, as the notion must be defended—over and over again—from the threats of simple reality. On the other hand, when we directly experience something—for example a tree—that's Buddhist emptiness. You are not separate from the tree; you are not labeling and conceptualizing it. You and the tree are one. No anxiety.

If we look at the Heart Sutra, *we see that emptiness is considered to be the absolute truth—no separation between the things of this world. For living beings there are no eyes, ears, nose, tongue, hand, no nothing because this reality is just functioning without any fixed entity; it is* empty.

In other words, the whole universe is just one thing, as five fingers are just one hand. Yet eyes are eyes, a nose is a nose, a tongue is a tongue, and a person is a person. So you see from one perspective that everything is different, and from another, you see that everything is the same. Our challenge is to see one reality from both sides. This is expressed in the Heart Sutra *as "form is emptiness and emptiness is form." As form everything is different, yet these forms are empty. Empty means there is no difference, yet this emptiness is form. What we see is the one reality as an intersecting or merging of oneness and uniqueness.*

"TRUE REALITY," 2012

The concept of dependent origination is the foundation for the understanding of emptiness. Whereas other philosophies and religions hold up something (often labeled a "soul") as uniquely separate from and independent of the rest of the world, Buddhism refuses to compromise. Each individual human being, no matter how much he or she believes there is some intrinsic self or soul or mind, is in reality just a temporary form that comes into being when conditions are right. And then, when the conditions for its existence change, what we have called the self changes into something else. We do not "go to heaven" as some recognizable "me" when we die. But then, from the Buddhist point of view, we never die and are never born because the parts that temporarily make up the self or "me" have no beginning and no end.

It's important to grasp this essential teaching on emptiness, both because it reveals the root cause of all our fear, anger, and grasping and because all the other things we've discussed—the various levels of consciousness, the skandhas, and the factors—only make sense if emptiness, dependent origination, is grasped. Don't worry if it doesn't make sense right away; just let it play in your mind as you go about your day, and you'll see evidence of it everywhere. Consider something as simple as an apple. In the Zen meal chant (*gatha*), we say, "Seventy-two labors brought us this food; we should know how it comes to us." Whether or not it is exactly seventy-two labors is not important; the point is to consider for a moment how many things come together to get an apple into your hands. First, the apple tree itself had to evolve over millions of years. Then, humans had to begin farming and learn to shape the kind of apples a tree produces. More recently, someone had to plant and tend the particular tree that produced that particular apple, and someone had to pick the apple and pack it for storage (unless you went apple picking!). Someone had to drive the truck over a road that countless people built and countless others use and maintain, and the truck itself had to be invented, built, bought, and fueled. And that's just for an apple! Imagine how complex the web of interdependence is to create a skyscraper, deliver chemotherapy to a cancer patient, or even to create the book you are reading right now.

This central teaching of emptiness due to the dependent arising of all things can become a tool for understanding, in a very fine-grained way, how people lock themselves into a view of their self and the world that is wholly based in delusion. In early Buddhism, practitioners created the concept of the twelve links of causation as a model for picturing the formation of such views and the actions that reinforce them. Originally, the twelve links explained how karma caused a person to be born, to develop cravings that led to more karma, and then to experience sickness, old age, and death—all the while generating new karma that will cause another cycle of rebirth and suffering.

Before we go on to explore the twelve links in detail, a word about rebirth. The Buddhist idea of rebirth is not reincarnation. The latter is the belief that something intrinsic and identifiable moves from a dying body to a new body (either one that has just been born or one that is about to be born). Reincarnation is utterly dependent on the belief that one's soul, self, or identity is unique and indestructible. Rebirth, on the other hand, sees the energy created by karma as what continues on, rather than any individual self. A way to think about this is to think about pool. A player doesn't hit the ball directly but, instead, hits the cue ball into the target ball. The energy from the cue ball transfers to the chosen ball and moves it forward, but that doesn't mean the chosen ball "becomes" the cue ball. Only the energy is carried forward. Another metaphor is lighting one candle with another. Does this mean that the second candle is the same as or a version of the first candle? No, and you can't even say the flame of the second candle "is" the flame from the first. (Are all fires the same fire? Yes and no!) When Zen Buddhists talk about rebirth, they are not contradicting the teaching about emptiness and impermanence of the self; nor is the traditional view of the twelve links, which refers to "three lives," suggesting that those lives belong in any intrinsic way to a unique identity. In any case, regardless of how you feel about rebirth, the twelve links are a psychologically nuanced and useful tool for understanding the ego.

THE TWELVE LINKS

The first link in the chain of dependent origination is ignorance. Normally *ignorance* means a lack of knowledge, but in Buddhism, it is closer to "ignoring." What is being ignored? Reality! The reality of emptiness, of the interrelated nature of all things. As soon as consciousness creates a self and dubs it unique, the chain has formed, and the unfolding of the links begins.

The Sanskrit word for the next link is *samskara*, which is variously translated as "mental formations" or "volitional activity." Because we are ignorant of the truth of things, we act in unskillful ways based on desires. In Zen, we chant the "Verse of Atonement," which says, in part, that karma is "born of my body, mouth, and thought," and that is one way to think about the second link. Whether through thoughts, speech, or actions, when we act out of our belief that we are separate from the rest of the world, we act in ways that have negative consequences.

The third link is consciousness, which is also the fifth skandha. Here it means the moment of awareness as a self, a separate being. The fourth link is "name + form" (*nama-rupa*), or, as we might say in modern terms, "mind-body." This is essentially the other four skandhas, the heaps or aggregates that make up everything. There is also a special meaning to the idea of rupa, beyond just the sense of the physical form it has in the skandhas. In the twelve links, rupa means an object that has been invested with meaning. For example, a chair is just a thing, but "Dad's chair" that no one else is allowed to sit in is a rupa. We invest a lot of things with meaning and use these things to create or shore up our sense of self—and in modern consumer culture, this is truer than ever before. Every time there's a natural disaster, people who have lost everything declare that their houses and possessions are just things and what matters is that the people are safe. No matter how many times we hear this repeated, we still attach to all kinds of things and believe that if we lose these things, we will lose parts of ourselves.

The fifth link is the six senses themselves (the five physical senses and the mind). And the sixth link is contact—the moment when we experience the input of our senses as pleasant, unpleasant, or neutral. As is true of this juncture in both the skandhas and the factors, the link between the sense experience and the evaluation of that experience as attractive or aversive is almost instantaneous. It's very hard to see that we *have* a reaction to a particular sight, sound, smell, or what-have-you, instead of the sight or sound *causing* the reaction. But, as mentioned in previous chapters, when we realize that two people react in opposite ways to the same experience, we also have to realize that the reaction is not embedded in the experience but arises from our engagement with that experience. And our engagement is based on our sense of self.

The fine distinctions between these links can be tricky, and it's not really necessary to be able to define exactly what is the moment of "nose-consciousness," what is the act of smelling, and what is the feeling tone of that smell. Just realize that these links explain that we move from general consciousness to focusing on a particular sensory experience. Out on a walk, for example, we can become aware of the smell of flowers and think, "Beautiful!" or the smell of gar-bage and think, "Ugh!" It's not really necessary for you to be able to break down this experience into links; just know that the chain is unfolding. And the other important thing to re-member about these first six links is that although the experi-ences of the senses often seem neutral at first, because of our consciousness of ourselves as separate from everything else, we move inevitably from sense perceptions to stories about those perceptions, as the next few links demonstrate.

The seventh link is feeling—that is, our emotional re-sponse to pleasant or unpleasant sensory experiences. The flowers make us want to stop and smell them more deep-ly; we feel happy or pleased with the moment. The garbage dump makes us walk faster; perhaps we feel a bit sick to our stomach, or we're sad that our walk was disrupted by some-thing ugly, or we're angry that there is so much waste. As we've discussed before, feelings in and of themselves are not a problem. But because we are conditioned to think that things "out there" cause our feelings, we therefore move in-evitably into ideas about those things that are incomplete or biased. Worst of all, such ideas lead us to believe our emo-tional reactions are outside our control and invested in the things (and people and events) around us.

The eighth link is craving. Craving can actually be posi-tive or negative—we crave more of things we have a pleasant response to, and we crave the eradication of things we find unpleasant. Craving, moreover, is desire without fulfillment, and this is what separates it from bodily necessities. One of my students offered this explanation: "If you'll eat carrots as happily as chocolate, you're really hungry, but if you only want the chocolate, you're having a craving."

Once we are trapped into craving, there naturally arises

the ninth link, clinging (sometimes called grasping or attachment). Clinging is a stronger form of craving—longer lasting, more desperate. This is when we really start to build a sense of identity around our desires and believe that we must have what we desire—that having is the only way to be content. The next link is called becoming, and it is here that we shift from recognizing desire as a feeling to believing it is part of who we are. Traditionally, this is the link that dictates rebirth, where the accumulated karma shapes the next life. Psychologically, however, it is the moment where we commit to an identity, a version of the self. And once we have done that, our ego consciousness automatically takes up the task of creating a sense of stability and continuity for that self. It's important to note that we don't commit to an identity just once, but over and over again. Sometimes, we consciously and deliberately commit to a new identity (becoming a parent, giving up smoking), but most often our sense of identity is recognized only in retrospect, after it has become an ingrained pattern.

The eleventh link is birth, and the twelfth is old age and death. At first, it seems very odd to have birth and death right next to each other, with nothing in between. Isn't everything we experience, think, and believe between these two moments? It seems like birth should be link one, not eleven! However, what the Abhidharma is pointing out is that once karma has been created, a new existence is inevitable, and that new existence must just as inevitably decay and die. What happens to individuals between those moments is not as important as the cycle itself.

Traditionally, birth here is understood as the literal birth of a new body, and death to be the literal death of that body. In contemporary Zen practice, it may be more useful to think that these two links describe the creation and then loss of an identity, a self-construction. The other way to understand "old age and death" is not the loss of the identity but the damage that identity causes. For example, if someone firmly believes "I am a smoker," he will feel unable to give up smoking, even as he develops a hacking cough and then lung cancer. The need to cling to the identity—and the stability that identity provides—is stronger than the desire to have a healthy body. Sometimes the consequences of the identity don't seem negative and can even seem positive and healthy. Much of Western psychology (and all of the self-help industry) is devoted to discarding unhealthy, damaging identities and building or strengthening healthy, positive identities. There is nothing wrong (and a good deal that is right) about starting an exercise program, learning to create loving relationships, or giving up bad habits. But this is still rearranging deck chairs on the Titanic—no matter how healthy, successful, and loved you are, you will still have suffering in your life, and you will still die. The twelve links point to the truth that there is absolutely no way to avoid the suffering that clinging and identity formation cause.

The twelve links are a very complex understanding of how the identity of the self is created, how that in turn creates karma, and how that karma influences future events. The skandhas trace much the same path in a more manageable level of detail, and several of the steps in the twelve links (such as form, sensation, and attachment) are the same as the skandhas. So, as I have said, it's not important to understand the nuances of each link in its original context. What I would like to do is describe a psychological understanding of the links. Instead of seeing the twelve links as only related to life as a whole—how craving and clinging inevitably lead to suffering through sickness, old age, and death—we can see them as describing how the same process creates our individual worldviews and shapes our sense of who we are as people.

This is easiest to see if we start not with the first link but with the fourth—form. As I said earlier, this is not just any physical thing but a thing that you consider linked to your sense of self. Think of something you consider important to how you define your identity, how you understand who you are. It could be your house or car. It could even be a person in your life—a partner or a child. For this example, let's use something simple—chocolate.

Chocolate by itself is neutral, neither good nor bad. Nor is there anything wrong with enjoying chocolate! But if we cling to the pleasure of chocolate and make it part of our identity, that identification becomes problematic. Once we identify as "a chocoholic," several things happen. First, we place our happiness in an external object. Second, we define our "self" in part through chocolate and our interaction with chocolate. Third, we start to view the world and shape our actions around this identity. This might seem overblown, but how many people want to lose weight or be healthier and then "can't" because of a powerful sense of loss and anxiety? It's not just giving up the chocolate that's painful; it's giving up the identification of self that seemed real and permanent.

If something as simple as craving a chocolate bar can set off suffering, how much more intense is that suffering if a more central identification is challenged? When emotions are painful and out of control—anger, fear, jealousy, anxiety— we can be sure that what is happening is a threat to some part of our sense of self. The twelve-linked chain is wrapped around us and pulling tighter and tighter! At its worst, the need to believe a worldview created by the ego can be so strong and the fear of having that worldview challenged so painful that we can lash out with violence and hate. When neo-Nazis believe that white people are under attack and that the only way to protect their way of life is to kill people of different races, this is the ego protecting a worldview at all costs. But it's important to understand that we all get caught in this level of belief, not just Nazis! "I am a defender of white culture, under attack and fighting to protect my people" and "I am a liberal who believes in diversity and the rule of law" have obvious, real-world differences. But in terms of the absolute, they are both equally flawed views, because *neither self exists* in any essential or fixed way. Creating identities that polarize us is always based in a failure to see both sides of reality—the relative and the absolute. Although you are not me and I am not you, we are the same. We are all part of the One Body that makes up everything, and the more we try to discriminate, the more damage we do.

This can be a very hard concept to grasp fully. It's much easier to see some parts of ourselves and our world as "good" and some parts as "bad," to believe that protecting and keeping the former and rejecting or stamping out the latter is the way to both a better world and lasting happiness. But it's simply not true. I want to stress that accepting reality as it is does not mean never trying to change anything or help anyone. Reducing the suffering of the world is compassion—wisdom in action—and it is part of the bodhisattva vows. But that still doesn't mean that those actions are intrinsically part of who you are. As an analogy, think about eating. What you eat can make a great deal of difference to your long-term health as well as your short-term mood, but that does not mean that the food you eat "is" you in some intrinsic way. Some of the food gets absorbed into your body, some gets passed out through the digestive system, but in no case does anyone ever look at a chocolate bar or a piece of bread and think, "That is me." We all know the food we eat is part of a constantly changing system. That's why we need to eat regularly—if it were otherwise, we would choose a healthy, nourishing meal one time and be done with it! In the same way, no accomplishment, work, relationship, or belief is really "us"; they're also all part of a constantly changing system, one that just does a better job of pretending to be static and permanent.

At this point you may be wondering: If there's no essential self, if everything is empty and impermanent, and if clinging to anything (even good things) just leads to suffering, how the heck do we ever find happiness, contentment, and balance? For over two thousand years, Buddhists have believed that meditation is the answer to that question, and for Zen students in particular, zazen is the central aspect of practice. I believe this is true. But I also believe that the world today is infinitely more complex—and even more neurotic—than the world of Shakyamuni Buddha. And therefore, I believe that bringing the modern tools of psychological understanding to our practice can help our zazen be successful. That is where working with the I-System comes in. The I-System can help create a bridge from our current way of thinking to the radical ideas of the Abhidharma and the twelve links.

SUMMARY OF THE TWELVE LINKS

It can be hard to hold the individual links clearly in your mind. While it is not necessary to have them all clearly distinguished, Buddhist texts often used pictures to summarize each link. Here is a verbal description of the common pictures used to help people understand and remember the links.

1. *Ignorance*: A blind man, who, in his state of ignorance, easily loses his way.

2. *Mental formations*: A potter, whose creations represent deeds and actions.

3. *Consciousness*: A monkey, representing the chatter of the untrained mind.

4. *Name + form*: A boat rocking with physical and spiritual instability.

5. *Six senses*: An empty house with six windows.

6. *Invested contact*: A lusty couple, embracing the object of desire.

7. *Sensation*: A man with an arrow in his eye, wounded by emotion.

8. *Craving*: A person drinking wine, dreaming of a desired object.

9. *Clinging*: A person holding one object and yet reaching for another.

10. *Becoming*: A pregnant woman, the life we create through craving.

11. *Birth*: The newborn baby representing the created identity.

12. *Decay and death*: An old person, limping toward the grave.

4

THE SIX REALMS

The last Buddhist psychological model from the Abhidharma I would like to introduce is the six realms. In classic Buddhist thinking, the realms are places of rebirth. Based on its karma, every sentient being is reborn into one of the realms. But even if you don't believe in rebirth, the six realms are a useful metaphor for our own states of mind. From this point of view, the realms are fluid states, and we inhabit each one repeatedly over the course of our life, or even over the course of a day! Recognizing what realm we inhabit in reaction to an event or a feeling can help us let go of the effects of that realm because we can gain distance from our feelings and see that they are transitory states, not reality. The realms are also useful because they deal with good states as well as bad ones, attractive as well as aversive reactions. It is easy, even seductive, to fall into the belief that what we should be trying to achieve is the eradication of bad feelings or events. Not only is this impossible, it is not the goal of practice. As Zen students, we strive to be calmly present for what is, not to force the world or our minds into a specific mode. The fact is the so-called good realms are no more the path to awakening and contentment than the so-called bad ones—a truth worth keeping in mind.

The first realm is the god (deva) realm. In Buddhist cosmology the god realm is populated with beings of great wealth and power who live long lives full of pleasure, surrounded by splendor and beauty. You're probably thinking, "Sign me up!" And in fact, one or another version of the god realm is the ideal in many cultures. Modern capitalist cultures, especially, tend to hold out wealth and pleasure as the best possible life and therefore what we should all want and strive for. But this realm is actually a trap. First of all, the devas are not immortal—they sicken and die like all beings. No matter how much money you accumulate, no matter how many toys you collect or how much power you have, you, like every other being, will die. What's more—before you die, you will likely grow old, suffer sickness, and lose loved ones and treasured possessions. The god realm is the Buddhist reminder that accumulating power and possessions is not the way out of suffering and that trying to create a life of pure pleasure is doomed to failure.

Second, Buddhism teaches that living in the god realm blinds us to the suffering of others and makes wisdom and compassion impossible. Unfortunately, this truth is very starkly on display in modern American society. Without wisdom and the compassion to help others, we cannot ever awaken. It is certainly possible to be wealthy and compassionate, but the protections provided by a life of privilege do tend to insulate us from suffering. We quite literally see less of the world's suffering, so it's easier to ignore, and we can also fall into the belief that we deserve the safety and pleasure we have more than others. Whether or not we worked hard for our nice home in a safe neighborhood is immaterial, because whatever we have we will lose one day. The seeming stability of a deva life is not the answer. Instead, as we age and sicken, we become more and more aware of the emptiness of a life focused on material goods, but we are unable to find the strength to change because we have become so used to placing our happiness in outside objects.

Finally, on a psychological level, the god realm is the realm of indolence and addiction. The relentless focus on pleasure as the answer to suffering can lead to overindulgence in and dependence on drugs, alcohol, food, shopping, or sex. When we numb out in front of the TV or social media, we are in the god realm, believe it or not. This realm is also the realm of pride, the kind of pride that needs to flaunt success or superiority to create self-worth. All of these experiences, as enjoyable as they are, facilitate our hiding from the reality of impermanence. But we cannot hide forever, and when we are forced to face reality, this realm leaves us completely unprepared.

A final point—the god realm is the realm of enjoying and valuing beauty of all kinds. It's important to stress that here, and in all the realms, the experiences or reactions *themselves* are not the cause of suffering. It's clinging to these experiences, believing that experiences or things are necessary for happiness, that leads to suffering. There is absolutely nothing wrong with being moved by a beautiful piece of music or wanting to have a lovely home. (After all, most books on meditation tell you to start by creating a calm, uncluttered, inviting space.) But if you can't meditate unless you are in your lovely space or if you can only enjoy something when it is new and flawless, you have moved into clinging to beauty in a problematic way.

The next realm is the demigod (asuras) realm. Asuras are powerful, long-lived beings who lack any morality and fight among themselves and with the devas, striving to take what they can and destroy what they cannot. This is the realm of envy, jealousy, and anger, as well as arrogance and paranoia (which sound like opposites but are actually two sides of the same coin). Sound familiar? Many of us spend an unfortunate amount of time in this realm. American culture, in many ways, is itself a product of the demigod realm.

When we are jealous of our romantic partners or envy friends their success, we are in the realm of the asuras. When we lash out in anger, suffer from imposter syndrome, or worry that no one likes us, we are in the realm of the asuras. And when we feel powerful because we perceive that we are above someone else, we are in the realm of the asuras. Although the animal realm (see below) is the official realm of fear, it's important to understand that the anger and grasping for power that are hallmarks of the demigod realm are just fear turned outward in an aggressive manner. We hate someone or something because we fear that it is a threat to us. We fail to recognize that this is ego talking—the desperate attempt by our consciousness to create a stable sense of self by defining everything not us as "other" (different, therefore bad, therefore to be rejected, controlled, even crushed). This realm uses up more energy than any other realm. It is an exhausting state wherein the self drives itself forward in an unending search for more and more proof of its own superiority and value.

There is one last important point to make about the demigod realm. When people with privilege feel that their privilege is threatened, they inhabit this realm. In recent years there has been a great deal of discussion about *privilege,* a word used to describe unearned benefits or advantages available only (and automatically) to some people. Although this definition of the term has been around since the turn of the twentieth century, it came to modern prominence in 1989, when writer and activist Peggy McIntosh wrote an article listing forty-six ways in which she, a white person, had privilege, including such things as, "If a traffic cop pulls me over, I can be sure I haven't been singled out because of my race."[7] Since this article was published, a great deal of scholarship has been done, and the idea that some people are privileged while others are not has been widely accepted. But people who have historically had privilege (in the United States, for example, privileged groups include men, white people, and Christians) often lash out in anger at the idea that they have unearned advantages. Not uncommonly, they come to believe that they are actually the ones under attack. For example, the attempt to recognize a variety of winter holidays led some Christians to declare there was a "war on Christmas." This kind of overreaction to a perceived threat, especially an existential threat, is very much part of the demigod realm. Much of the division and anger in our culture can be explained through the realization that for demigods, sharing is an impossible concept—this mind-set can only see that as loss, even if the thing being shared is something limitless, like equality or love.

The third realm is the human realm. It can be a little odd to think of the human realm as a psychological state—aren't we all human all the time? In Buddhist cosmology, the human realm is the only state in which a being can awaken. So, psychologically, the human realm is the realm of desire, doubt, and passion. These can be good or bad drives, depending on what they are aimed at. As I mentioned in the chapter on the omnipresent factors, desire is not in and of itself bad (a common misunderstanding of Buddhism); what matters is clinging to that desire as a source of identity and happiness.

So, in the human realm, desire that is held lightly, out of love or compassion, is good desire. The object of the desire or passion is not what matters. Consider an activist, for example—imagine someone who is passionate about doing good, perhaps fighting against child abuse. While we can all agree that child abuse is something that should be stopped, there is a great deal of difference between someone who takes up this cause out of hatred for child abusers, who wants to punish them and sees them as nothing but evil, and someone who takes up the cause out of compassion for both the children and their abusers. The person who clings to the need to change the laws or punish the abusers, who feels that life will be worthless unless this fight is won, is in a very different place from someone who understands that she may not be able to make all the changes she wants to see but is willing to do what can be done. Finally, a person who demonizes the abusers will never understand that most abusers were themselves abused as children and that compassion and a chance to heal are a necessary part of ending the cycle. When you are motivated to create change or achieve something, you are always in the human realm, but it is always important to examine your motives.

It is interesting to think about what it means that the human realm is the realm of doubt. Mind states in other realms often evince a false sense of certainty and permanence—when we are in the hell realm, we don't question our anger and hatred; we just inhabit it. When we are in the grip of an addiction in the god realm, we don't question the need to satisfy the craving. Later, when we wonder why we got so very angry or why the craving was so powerful, we enter the human realm. This is the mental and emotional state where change can happen. When we are in the human realm, we are in the best position to examine our motives and choose how we engage with ourselves and the world.

The next three realms are sometimes called the lower realms, and it is easy to look at the descriptions and think they are the "bad" realms. That would be a mistake. When the goal is to wake up, the god realm is as bad, as much of a trap, as the hell realm. I cannot stress enough that we do not practice Zen in order to be happier more often. If that is your goal, I suggest exercise or getting a pet. Zen is a reorientation of your entire view of reality; the goal is not to escape the hell or hungry ghost realms but to be aware of what's happening when we end up there, to be present for the hate or the craving, and to let go of those mind states rather than trying to fix them.

Before talking about these realms, I want to stress again that we all move in and out of all these states all the time. These realms are not just for those who are diagnosed with mental illnesses such as depression or anxiety. If you slip into road rage when you get cut off, you are in the hell realm, even if you are there for only a minute or two. One form of resistance that is common is to see these realms as momentary states we slip into and not "the real me." In one way, of course, that's true—because there is no "real me." But immediately excusing oneself for lashing out or cheating by having the thought "That's not what I'm like" is, in I-System terms, a fixer. It is a form of psychological resistance.

The animal realm is the realm of sensual craving, fear, and ignorance. Humans, of course, are animals, and thus we all spend a great deal of time in this realm, whether we recognize it or not. Furthermore, the three aspects of this realm are more complicated than they first seem, so let's explore them one at a time.

First, sensual craving. In the modern United States, we often conflate "sensual" and "erotic," so it is important to remember that sensual simply means "of the senses." The taste of chocolate, the smell of lavender, the feel of a warm blanket, the sound of a favorite song, the beauty of a natural landscape—all of these are sensual pleasures. Sensuality is not bad, but sensual craving is. Craving sensual experiences and clinging to them means believing that these things are necessary for happiness, and it also means we will devote our time and energy to seeking out these pleasures.

Because the animal realm is the realm of instinctive responses, it is a realm of fear. When we are in this realm, we are motivated by fear of discomfort. Like an animal building a den, we seek to create a life that is safe, familiar, and protected. And while we all need to retreat to a place of safety sometimes, habitually responding to anything new by withdrawing from or rejecting it means we live small, stifled lives. In addition, our instinctive reactions are conditioned by our surroundings, and this means the animal realm is the realm of prejudice and bigotry.

Finally, it is important to remember that in Buddhist psychology, ignorance (as I discussed in the chapter on the twelve links) is actually *ignoring*. It doesn't carry the Western meaning of simple lack of knowledge; instead, it means the willful rejection of reality in favor of the comforting delusions of self, permanence, and external happiness. The animal realm is the realm of ignorance because it is the realm we slip into when we refuse to face the world as it is. In other words, every time we say, "I know this is bad for me, but I just don't care," we are in the animal realm.

Before we talk about what the realm of the hungry ghost signifies, let me explain what a hungry ghost is. These are pathetic beings that have huge, empty bellies but tiny mouths and long, very skinny necks so that they cannot swallow. Thus, they are perpetually starving, desperate for food but unable to feed themselves. And because they are ghosts, they cannot die and escape the torment of their hunger. During retreats, at the midday meal, we make an offering to the hungry ghosts, as a symbolic gesture of our vow to save all sentient beings and our compassion for the suffering of those beings.

With this description, the psychological aspect of the hungry ghost realm is probably obvious—it is the realm of intense craving, greed, and dissatisfaction. Not actual addictions—remember that is part of the god realm—but the craving for something that leads to addiction definitely belongs here. Whenever we feel an intense desire that is not tied to an actual physiological need, we are in the hungry ghost realm. So actual hunger is not part of this realm, but an overwhelming craving for a particular food or the feeling that you have to keep eating even after physical hunger is gone—that's a hungry ghost mentality. Although all the realms are tied to what in the I-System are called fixers (the belief that there is something "out there," outside ourselves, that will create happiness and well-being), the hungry ghost realm is where the role of fixers is most obvious. I find that many people spend a lot of time in the hungry ghost realm, always craving *something* to fill them up and give them contentment or a sense of purpose. People want to fix their lives, but by that they mean "acquire things/accomplishments/roles/relationships that will distract me from this gnawing sense of emptiness."

One of my students has suggested that this realm is also the one we inhabit when we are depressed. This might at first seem counterintuitive. Depression, after all, is commonly understood as a critical lack of desires or feelings. But depression is what happens when the weight of dissatisfaction and overwhelming but unmet desire turns inward. The crushing certainty that happiness and well-being are impossible is what happens when hungry ghost thoughts are so powerful they paralyze. Think again about the image of a hungry ghost—the huge belly and the tiny mouth and throat. When people are depressed, nothing they experience makes a difference, just as no amount of food a hungry ghost can actually get down its throat can make a difference. Here the hungry ghost is not connected to fixers, but rather to depressors— the mind telling us that nothing will ever change or get better, so we should give up.

Finally, it's useful to recognize that the hungry ghost is a demigod without any power. I'm not talking about actual power to effect change in the world, but instead a belief in one's power. When people have an intense craving and believe they should or do have the ability (or worse, right) to have that craving fulfilled, any hindrance or delay will lead to lashing out, to anger based on envy or entitlement. On the other hand, if they feel an intense craving but also feel they have no personal control over getting that craving met, they will subside into dissatisfaction and depression. Both these realms are the realms of unmet cravings, just as the god realm and the animal realm are the realms where cravings are temporarily satiated and keeping that satisfied feeling becomes the focus.

Finally, we come to the hell realm. In Christianity, hell is the place where bad people suffer unending torment. The Sanskrit word for this realm is *naraka*, which originally meant the underworld. Since it is a place of punishment in both Hinduism and Buddhism, it is perfectly reasonable to translate *naraka* as "hell," so long as we remember there are two important differences from the Christian hell. First, we do not end up in the hell realm because we have been judged by some divine being; we send ourselves there. Second, hell in Buddhist cosmology is not eternal (although it can feel that way!); it is a psychological state we move in and out of just like all the other realms.

Hell is the realm of hatred and intense aggression. It is worth noting that Buddhist psychology separates anger and hatred, seeing them as separate realms and psychological states. Anger flashes out quickly, in response to a particular event or interaction. Hatred, on the other hand, seethes and lingers. Anger makes us feel powerful; hatred makes us feel powerless—it is a feeling we do not believe we can escape. Hate is also the hardest feeling to see as arising from within us. When people hate, they believe it is because of what someone or something else has done *to* them and that the hate is an inevitable response to mistreatment and injustice. It can be very hard to see that hatred is still a choice we make, not an uncontrollable reaction.

This is not to suggest that there are not bad things in the world or that we should be OK with anything that happens, no matter how much pain or suffering it causes. Another common misconception of Buddhism is that Buddhists strive to be "above it all," floating on a fluffy pink cloud, untouched by anything bad. This is not true for any Buddhist and is especially not true for Zen Buddhists, who vow to follow the path of the bodhisattvas—to save all sentient beings. It is true that there is great injustice and suffering in the world, but it is equally true (if harder to accept) that hatred never creates the condition for positive change. Hatred is, by its very nature, destructive.

The final point to make about the hell realm is to reiterate that we all visit it. We often want to reserve the hell realm for those few people who have done things so awful that we can define them as evil—mass shooters, for example. But to reduce the hell realm to this select group entails resistance to looking at ourselves truthfully. We have all hated someone or something, even if we didn't act on that hate or the hate burned itself out. When we dwell on how an ex-partner was a horrible person, we are in the hell realm, even if (and this is most important) our ex-partner *was* a horrible person. To escape from hell, we need to see that hate is still hate even if the target of that hate deserves it—because, in the end, hatred burns the one who hates, not the one who is hated.

I would like to make two final points. The first is that, while we all move in and out of these realms over and over, we do tend to have one or maybe two "home realms." Some people respond aggressively to any perceived discomfort, while others automatically look for a way to self-soothe. It's important to think about what realm or realms you operate out of most of the time, because identifying patterns (or, in the language of the I-System, story lines) is the first step toward dismantling them.

The second point is that, although I have listed the realms in a particular order, that order does not represent an inherent structure; nor should you think that the realms are ranked best to worst. We don't move from one realm to another in any progressive way, climbing from hell to hungry ghost to animal and so on. And while the human realm is traditionally the realm where awakening happens, this does not mean that you are doomed if you identify your home realm as, for example, the hungry ghost realm. It simply means that when you are in the human realm, you are in a state where you can focus on letting go of that particular form of clinging and being present for what is.

SUMMARY OF THE REALMS

God realm—indolence, pleasure, comfort, lack of compassion, addiction.

Demigod realm—jealousy, anger, arrogance, aggression, desire for power.

Human realm—doubt, passion, change.

Animal realm—sensual craving, fear, ignorance (reacting instinctively).

Hungry ghost realm—intense craving, greed, dissatisfaction, depression.

Hell realm—hatred and intense aggression.

Some definitions of karma suggest that it is fixed and predetermined. But from a Buddhist perspective, karma is more like an accumulation of tendencies that can lock us into particular behavior patterns that themselves result in further accumulations of those tendencies. Thus, when we speak of a person's karma, it means the sum total of the person's direction in life and the flow of things that occur around that person, all caused by antecedent conditions, actions, thoughts, feelings, and desires.

So, as you can see, it is easy to become imprisoned by our karma and to think that the cause of our life not working (or not working as well as we would like) lies elsewhere—with conditions beyond our control.

The good news is that we don't have to be trapped by our karma. When we sit, we are not allowing our impulses to translate into action—we are just watching them. Looking at impulses, we see that they arise and pass away and that they are not us, and we do not have to be ruled by them.

"What Is Karma," 2013

5

THE I·SYSTEM

The rest of this book focuses on psychological work in a spiritual context. This is not to say that there isn't a place for psychotherapy. But as John Welwood discusses in *Toward A Psychology of Awakening*, whenever we work on ourselves with a particular outcome in mind, whenever we strive to get somewhere different from where we are, we cut ourselves off from the present moment—which is the only true agent of healing and transformation that there is. With the exception of the I-System and the gestalt model, which foster unconditional presence, psychotherapeutic models focus on establishing healthy boundaries—between self and other or between mind and body. But Zen teaches that there are no boundaries and thus reveals the delusion of the separate, independent self.

Even though this is not a book about psychotherapy, clearly I am advocating for a practice that includes psychological awareness. Why is that the case? Welwood also points out that in our culture, which is much more complex than the culture of Shakyamuni Buddha, there is an epidemic of people who are unable to find a space for their practice because they don't have the cultural support. For centuries, throughout India and Asia, there has been a tradition of both separate spaces (such as monasteries) and cultural support (such as offering *dana*) for those who wish to devote themselves to practice. The West, and especially the United States, does not have such a tradition and in fact looks suspiciously on those who wish to step away from capitalism and individuality. So it can be difficult to practice regularly and deeply, no matter how dedicated you are.

Dependent origination, the skandhas, the factors, and the realms all describe different facets of the same process— namely, the process by which one gets tangled up in suffering and angst through mental conditioning. It is our clinging, our wanting things to be other than they are, that causes our suffering. And this suffering arises from all the work we do to create and maintain a stable sense of self—the constant, natural effort of the self to discriminate, both between "self" and "not-self" and between what it finds pleasant or valuable and what it finds unpleasant or worthless. As Caroline Brazier says in *Buddhism on the Couch*, "Self is a defensive prison of habit-energy . . . and the teaching of non-self invites you to step beyond this prison into vibrant relationship with life."[8] I would add that many people claim to want to escape the prison of suffering, but what they really want is a more comfortable cell—pictures on the wall, a big-screen TV. It can be scary to let go of the craving for material success and worldly esteem, but you can't learn to fly if you never let go of your seat!

Because it can be so hard to really let go of the notion of a stable, separate self, the I-System can be a useful complement to and first step toward successful zazen. Like meditation, the I-System aids in the deconditioning of the mind-set that creates suffering. However, the I-System has two elements that make this approach more palatable to many of us in the modern world. First, it's more concrete and tangible—doing a mind map yields immediate information that is based in physical reactions but that can also be processed intellectually. By contrast, sitting, in most cases, only very gradually frees the mind and changes worldviews. And although an important aspect of Zen training is to let go of the need to rely on the small mind of rational thought, this takes time and can be hard to do. The slow nature of Zen sitting and the difficulty of relinquishing one's reliance on rational thought can cause frustration and lead to the abandonment of practice before any real benefit is apparent.

Second, the I-System enables one to measure one's progress. This is in direct contrast to zazen and Zen in general, which views striving for measurable goals as just another trap. Returning to a mind map in a week or a month quantifies change in a very satisfying way and makes the "goalless goal" of Zen easier to accept. In my decades of teaching, I have found that many people give up on meditation, perhaps Zen in particular, because they don't believe that they're getting anywhere and come to see the practice as a waste of time. Our culture values speed—we want our dinner out of the microwave in two minutes, our workouts done in twenty minutes, and our phones to connect to the internet instantly all the time. Audio books even come with a feature to play at one and a half times normal speaking speed, so we can listen "faster." With that mentality, it's no surprise that meditation can start to feel like a waste of time. Indeed, unscrupulous marketers have used this frustration to market "quick" and "easy" meditations that promise not just relaxation (which can be achieved fairly rapidly) but mindfulness or even enlightenment. Doing mind maps does not speed up the process of awakening, but it's a way for us modern, psychologically attuned Westerners to get more traction on that path. Mind maps can help us see the progress we are making and therefore make the long, slow path of zazen easier to stick to.

The I-System can help us integrate spiritual realization into our busy lives; meditation practice helps us remain calm with the ups and downs of life. Together, the two offer a practice that can work better than either alone. And the combination is especially useful to those who do not have regular access to a dharma teacher. Without a guide, the path to nonself can be tricky indeed, and while I would never suggest that the I-System or this book can replace a teacher, I recognize that not everyone can meet weekly or even monthly with someone who has trained for decades and understands how to help others navigate a Zen practice. The ego is stubborn and tricky; it is quite willing to pretend it has dissolved if that is what consciousness claims it wants. Using the I-System theory with the practical tool of mind maps can provide some basic feedback about whether what you are experiencing is clarity or just another type of delusion.

Before going further into the mind maps, I want to remind you once again that both the Abhidharma and the I-System are models, not truths. As with all models, they can only describe reality in partial ways. They may be useful for many people and in many situations, but they are not the only tools; nor are they guaranteed to work. As a number of Zen masters have pointed out, even naming reality is an act of description and therefore an act of separation. That means we are not encountering reality itself but a concept of it. So please don't get caught up in the belief that this is "The Method." It's only *a* method—but one I hope you find helpful.

MIND MAPS AND ABHIDHARMIC MODELS

In the following pages, you will find mind maps that are linked to the psychological models from the Abhidharma we've studied in this book, and I will also suggest ways in which specific elements of the I-System correlate to specific aspects of the Abhidharma. These are not exact matches, and it is important to recognize that the I-System elements connect to more than the one aspect I have suggested, but I have found it useful to map one onto the other, especially as a way to get started. I will go into much more detail in each section, but here is an overview.

The skandhas (chapter 6), which describe how a self is built up, correspond most closely to the I-System aspect of requirements—the things or situations we think we need to feel happy and safe. This is where the most basic but important map is explored: "Who am I?" This is a map worth returning to time and again because seeing how the answers to the question change, we start to let go of the idea that the self is fixed or permanent. Another map you will find in this chapter is "How I should be." This map follows up on where we think we are with where we think we should be.

The omnipresent factors (chapter 7), which describe in detail how our reactions to external events occur, correspond to the I-System fixers and depressors. The factors describe the way we move from having a sensory experience to fitting that experience into a preexisting pattern. Fixers and depressors, similarly, are about patterns that seem very powerful, due to the mistaken belief that happiness depends on conditions outside ourselves being a certain way. Fixers respond to an experience (or even the idea of an experience) by trying to change what happened or will happen.

Depressors respond to an experience by asserting that the event is part of a static pattern and cannot be changed. Whether your Identity-System leans toward using fixers or depressors (although everyone uses both to some extent), the goal is the same—to shift responsibility for a mental state to the outside world. The maps here are "What do I need to be happy?" and "How my world should be."

Dependent origination (chapter 7) is about the way identities and worldviews form, and thus it corresponds to the I-System aspect of story lines. Just as the twelve links describe the step-by-step process of *becoming* (in all senses of the word), story lines empower and charge the Identity-System by supporting the belief that everything is a pattern that fits together. Most of us are very uncomfortable with the idea that our lives contain a great deal of randomness, so we retroactively create stories around things that happen in order to maintain the illusion of control. "Everything happens for a reason" is the most familiar example of story line thinking. The map "How did I get to be the way I am?" is a powerful and flexible map that can be focused on an aspect of life: "How did I get to be the way I am in relationships?" or "How did I get to be so afraid of risks?" are just two examples of how this map can be focused. Maps related to the factors and the links are in one chapter since both of these describe the way the ego relates to outside conditions.

Each of the six realms (chapter 8) gets its own maps, since each realm describes a specific psychological state. In each case, the goal is to explore what the realm offers you and what keeps you stuck there. In this chapter, instead of focusing mainly on one part of the Identity-System, we'll put the parts together. After you do a realm map, questions will guide you through considering the requirements:

God realm—What beautiful things do I wish for? What am I addicted to?

Demigod realm—How do I defend my happiness? Who or what am I jealous of?

Human realm—What specific goals do I dwell on? How am I going to improve my life?

Animal realm—What am I afraid of?

Hungry ghost realm—What do I hunger for? What makes me dissatisfied with life?

Hell realm—What makes me angry?

In the next map chapter (chapter 9), I have included a variety of maps specific to Zen practice. These can be used as an adjunct to the above maps (as a way to further explore clinging to the self), when you hit a rough patch in your sitting, or both. These maps are designed with a focus on meditation practice, but they can certainly be used to explore resistance to or concerns with other parts of your life. Finally, in chapter 10, I have offered a few words on some of the key sutras (teachings of the Buddha) along with mind maps that can show you how to bring these powerful texts into your day-to-day life.

I have, over the years, created these Zen-specific maps for my students; the other maps are used with permission of Stanley Block, who created the I-System. If you find mind maps helpful, I highly recommend exploration of Mind-Body Bridging. Stanley Block has written a number of workbooks targeting specific problems, such as anger, addiction, and PTSD, which go into greater detail.[9]

Within all beings there exists the buddhadhatu—*the "buddha-element" or "buddha-principle." Buddhadhatu is the utterly pure, unconditional, inviolate, indestructible, steadfast, and unshakeable eternal buddhic essence of all sentient beings. It is the life force, the nurturing power within us that sustains us, and when fully realized, it can transform us into a buddha.*

This true self is complete within every being, but it is hidden deep inside. Perception of buddha-nature is obtained by clearing away all the kleshas *(negative mental states and tendencies), such as greed, anger, ignorance, pride, and jealousy, which conceal it from view. The eradication of such emotional afflictions allows buddha-nature to stand revealed in all of its shining splendor. The major delusion we suffer from is to see self where there is in fact nonself and to see nonself where there is in reality the self (i.e., the unconditional buddha).*

This practice will transform our life but not be anything we think or figure out. It is by us giving up our ego-centered dreams of reality for who we really are—buddhas!

"ON THE NATURE OF THE SELF," 2014

6

INTERNAL MAPS
AND THE SKANDHAS

THE "WHO AM I?" mind map is a way of looking at the definition of self that is less complicated than the skandhas but also demonstrates how we identify with and attach to our notion of self. The core belief of our Identity-Systems is that the self is damaged and needs to be fixed. The goal of the mind maps is to uncover ways this belief manifests, as a first step in realizing it is not true and is in fact a figment of our imagination. In the I-System model, as in Zen, the self is not viewed as damaged because there simply is no self. Even on a relative or conventional level, the self is a process, always in flux, and in each moment it is exactly what it is. To think otherwise is dualistic, creating subject and object, or "good self" and "bad self."

What makes dualism a problem is that whenever you invoke something, you also invoke the opposite. As soon as you think, "I am a good person," you have invoked the idea of "a bad person," whether you mean to or not. It's like trying to imagine light without understanding what dark is—impossible! Because we come from a place of damage, as soon as the negative feeling shows up, we automatically try to recapture the positive feeling via the belief that we need external validation or that we need to change. But the only constant is change, so trying to hold on to one thing is doomed to failure. Striving for a goal, such as being good, is like running a race with a constantly moving finish line. You can never be good enough, so you never feel complete. The goal of spiritual practice is to be intimate with whatever is in the present moment, rather than trying to fix ourselves. We don't need to fix ourselves—we're not broken. And the main reason we're not broken is because the "I" doesn't actually exist.

A mind map takes what is often subconscious or implicit in our thinking and puts it down on paper, so the beliefs can be examined. The very process of writing down thoughts is an effective tool for weakening their hold on your reality, and the structure of mind mapping is even more effective than journaling.

Take a blank piece of paper, and draw a circle on it with the question "Who am I?" in the middle. Set a timer for three or four minutes, and start writing whatever comes to mind when you think about the prompt "Who am I?" Write your responses around the circle. Don't censor yourself or evaluate your answers as you're writing. If you draw a blank before the time is up, just write "blank" and keep going. Be especially careful not to evaluate your answers—don't put down what you think is the "right" answer or stop yourself from putting down something that seems silly. If "gardener" or "very neat" or "has to watch a TV show all the way through even if I stop liking it at season 3" comes up, that's important to your conception of who you are in this moment, and you should put it down.

WHO AM I?

BODY TENSION
Is your body tense or relaxed?
Where is the tension being held?
Is your mind cluttered or clear?

What do you notice about the things you wrote? Was the exercise easy or hard, or did it start out easy and then become more difficult? Just the act of describing who you think you are is a revealing exercise!

The next step is to understand the answers in terms of your requirements. Requirements are statements that contain "should" or "shouldn't" (or some variation like "must" or "ought") and describe rules your Identity-System has about how you (and the whole world) should be. Often, requirements are about the outside world—"Everyone should recycle," "My spouse shouldn't forget our anniversary"—but right now, we're going to focus on the rules we create for ourselves. These are intimately tied to our roles and identities and thus to the five skandhas.

Remember that the skandhas involve taking perceptions of physical and mental experiences, fitting them into a pattern, and using that pattern to establish a sense of stable ego or self. When we define who we are through roles (parent, teacher, Zen student) or identities (kind person, liberal), we are reaffirming the patterns and thus reaffirming the sense of self.

Now consider the various roles and identities you wrote down around the oval. Some of the roles probably make you feel happy, proud, or accomplished. Others probably make you feel threatened, inadequate, or ashamed. But the real question is, are these roles really *you*? From a Zen perspective, the answer, of course, is "no, because there is no *you*."

To make this clearer, consider how in the West and especially in the United States, we often define ourselves by our jobs. It's one of the first things we'll ask a new acquaintance: "What do you do?" Studies have shown that losing a job, and especially being unemployed for a long time, can cause anxiety, depression, and even suicidal thoughts. But how can our essential self be so wholly invested in something entirely outside of us? How can we lose our "self" when we lose our job? Both the I-System and Zen point out that investing a sense of safety and reality in things outside ourselves is doomed to failure because *everything* is impermanent. If you have a requirement that people recognize you as "a lawyer," "a parent," or "an organized person," you are bound to be disappointed at some point, either because you stop being a lawyer or because someone considers another aspect of your identity to be more important. Worse still, if we have a role we think is an important part of our identity, we are bound to disappoint ourselves at some point by failing to fulfill that role.

If you have a requirement for yourself that you should be "a loving person," then you are going to judge yourself, moment by moment, against that requirement. No one is loving *all the time*. But focus on these roles or identities, invest in them, make them requirements, and your ego—the consciousness created by the skandhas—will obediently measure everything you do and everything that happens against those requirements. This can create cognitive dissonance ("I'm *a loving person*, so if I cheat on my partner, it's because they don't appreciate my love and I can't help finding someone who does") or a sense of shame and damage for not living up to your self-imposed standards ("I wasn't loving in that interaction, so I guess I'm a bad person").

Example: Maria (a pseudonym) is one of the students in Soji's study group. One of the weeks we were studying the skandhas was also the week Maria found out she had been turned down for a promotion at work. While this would be upsetting for anyone, Maria was taking it very hard and felt it said something about who she "truly" was. I asked everyone to do a mind map with the prompt "Who am I?" This was Maria's map:

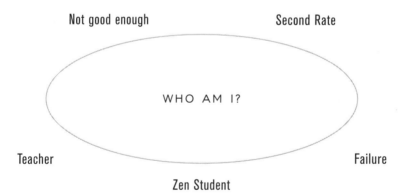

When it came time to list her requirements, Maria had no trouble coming up with a bunch: "I should be respected by my colleagues"; "I should be promoted"; "I should be a better teacher"; "I should work harder." Maria also admitted to feeling like a failed Zen student for caring so much about the promotion and not being able to let go of her desire for recognition. So another requirement was "I shouldn't be attached to recognition and success." Here's an example of how practice can cause more mental stress—it was one more piece of evidence proving her identity as a failure.

By reviewing the skandhas step by step (see chapter 1), Maria could understand that it's not that she was intrinsically a failure but that she had created this identity. Looking at the first skandha, she could see that the promotion, with the resulting nicer office and raise, was a rupa, a thing or form that she endowed with meaning. This is not to suggest that a promotion doesn't have real-world consequences—more money, different responsibilities, and so on. But in terms of defining the self, a promotion matters only if you let it. For Maria, the promotion was proof that she was respected by her colleagues and, furthermore, that she was worthy of that respect. The second and third skandhas, feeling and perception, are what endow the form, the promotion, with such intense meaning. Maria's perception of what the promotion meant *about her* hooked her into a pattern of association and created the craving for the promotion and all it represented. This craving naturally and immediately led to the fourth skandha, discrimination. Remember that this is the moment the mind rationalizes the understanding or choice made in the previous moment, the moment of perception. In Maria's case, the moment of discrimination was when she committed wholly to the belief that getting (or not getting) a promotion was part of a much larger pattern about whether she was valuable to and respected by others.

The fifth skandha is where the real danger of this cycle

becomes clear. This is where the story of the self as coherent, stable, and separate comes into being and also where that self, that identity, is protected. The fifth skandha is there to prop up the story line of the ego, regardless of how much anxiety or unhappiness it causes. Maria had invested strongly in the idea that the promotion would prove she was a respected teacher. In fact, she had invested so strongly that it was easier to believe she was a failure than to let go of the story line about the promotion. Because "being respected" had become the default pattern she used to shape everything that happened into a coherent identity, "I am not respected" was less disruptive (if more painful) to her sense of self than "being respected is not relevant to my identity."

Imagine the relief of letting go of the roles as actual parts of yourself (using the skandhas as a reminder of the Buddhist worldview of no-self) and instead lightly holding the roles as activities you have chosen to engage in for a time. They might be important and meaningful, but not defining. Imagine not being bound by requirements that are inflexible and therefore impossible. In Zen, we strive to drop all identities, to become "one true person of no rank" by recognizing that none of the identities are actually real, in the sense of being fixed and permanent. That can be a very challenging idea. One of the ways to begin approaching that idea is with the I-System technique called bridging.

Now you are going to do the same map again but this time with bridging. This is a technique that allows the Identity-System to rest by separating the present moment from the intensity of the requirements. Before you begin the map, make sure you are seated comfortably. Allow yourself to become aware of the present moment in an embodied way—feel the pressure of the chair on your back or thighs, feel the floor beneath your feet, become conscious of the weight of the pen, or listen to some background noise like a fan or a white-noise machine. Whatever you pick, the idea is to be gently aware—you aren't focusing intently on the sound or the pressure, but just letting it wash over your mind. Spend at least a few minutes attuning to your senses in this way, until you feel fully focused. Now write your responses to the "Who am I?" map again. They might turn out to be exactly the same, somewhat different, or totally different, but whatever you write, keep your focus on the sound or pressure instead of the feelings that come up when you write.

WHO AM I?

Did you notice a difference when you did the map with bridging? When you focus on the sensations, such as a background noise or the feel of your feet on the ground, you are in the present moment instead of being fully swept up in the Identity-System. To make clear how differently you feel after this map, you can answer the follow-up questions about mind clutter and body tension; hopefully you'll see that your answers are very different. The relaxation and lack of distress is because you are operating out of your Executive Function instead of your Identity-System. Executive Function is how the mind operates when you let go of the belief you are damaged and in need of fixing; it is the goal of Mind-Body Bridging.

Whereas Mind-Body Bridging focuses on bridging as the key step toward a healthier mental system, I see it as the first step toward achieving a state of positive samadhi (discussed in chapter 2), the state in which you become completely immersed in the present moment by focusing intently and utterly on something. People commonly achieve positive samadhi in zazen by focusing on the breath. Bridging allows for the development of one-pointed focus but requires a division of subject and object—no matter how much you focus on the sound of the fan or the feel of the chair, you are also, at the same time, writing, and thus your attention is split. The next step—positive samadhi—is to drop the external focus and instead focus on something within yourself. Eventually you will drop even that—drop everything—and enter the state of no-thought that is absolute samadhi. Just to be clear, samadhi is not the immediate next step after doing a mind map with bridging. It is a state that is achieved through a great deal of zazen. But you move toward this state by remembering the relaxed presence of bridging and then letting go even more fully, eventually dropping off not just mental chatter but body and mind itself.

Although we're going to talk about fixers and depressors in more detail in the next chapter, I want to introduce fixers here because they are so closely connected to internal requirements. If you go back to the first map and identify traits you see as negative, you will see what evokes the requirements—ideas of "how I should be" cause you to strive to be that ideal person. Of course, as noted before, this doesn't work, because you really aren't damaged, but the more you try to be "better," the more your mind will seek out mistakes, weaknesses, and failures for you to fix. Let's look at a map that helps you identify and understand fixers. Do the following map: "How I should be." Once again, quickly and without censoring yourself, write down anything that comes up in response to the prompt.

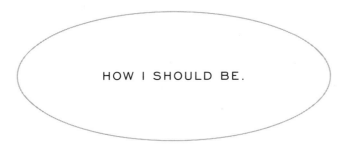

HOW I SHOULD BE.

Once you're finished, it's time to review your answers and your reactions to writing them.

BODY TENSION
Is your body tense or relaxed?
Where is the tension being held?
Is your mind cluttered or clear?
What are your requirements?

If you look at all the thoughts you have scattered around this map, you can very clearly see how you are living with conditions; you believe that certain things must be different before you can feel at peace. This is unsustainable. At Soji, we instruct people new to meditation that, once the period has started, they should not shift to find a more comfortable position nor scratch an itchy nose. The reason, we explain, has nothing to do with not distracting others or with some kind of endurance test. Instead, we point out that trying to make themselves comfortable means they are not accepting what actually is. ("If my nose would just stop itching, I could meditate in peace.") Then we ask, "If the only time you can be happy is when everything is exactly the way you want it, how often are you going to be happy?" The same thing is true here. If you are only at peace with the world when your conditions are met, how often will you be at peace?

Instead of trying to fix yourself by meeting a bunch of requirements, remember what you learned about the skandhas—you are not a single, unchanging entity, separate from the rest of the world, but rather aggregates of sensations and experiences that your mind groups into a coherent pattern and gives the identity of "me." And therefore nothing—no *thing* or behavior or belief—can ever give this identity the security it craves. Better to let go of it entirely! To practice doing that, try doing the map again with bridging.

HOW I SHOULD BE.

I hope doing this map with bridging lets you experience a greater sense of calm as you realize that being in the present moment and in your body demonstrates that right here, right now, you don't have need of any requirements, and there is nothing to fix. Just as the skandhas are about our internal sense of self, requirements are about what we think we need to have to feel whole and happy. In the next chapter, we'll look at fixers and depressors in more detail, and we'll relate them to the omnipresent factors and the twelve links of dependent origination.

7

EXTERNAL MAPS, OMNIPRESENT FACTORS, AND DEPENDENT ORIGINATION

As we discussed earlier, the skandhas describe the internal creation of a self, while the omnipresent factors and dependent origination describe how the self builds an identity through interaction with external factors. In terms of the I-System, I've linked the skandhas to requirements, beliefs about what should be, which activate the Identity-System. In this chapter I'll introduce maps about fixers and depressors and link those to the omnipresent factors. I'll also consider story lines and how they connect to the chain of dependent origination. But I want to make clear that the division I'm making (on the one side, skandhas/requirements/internal, and on the other, factors and dependent origination/fixers, depressors, and story lines/external) is for clarity and ease of presentation. The factors can easily be connected to requirements—certainly we all have beliefs about the world as well as about ourselves! In the same way, fixers and depressors can be purely about self-identity, although most often they are about how we relate to the rest of the world. Please don't feel you have to rigidly force your responses into internal and external just because that is how I have chosen to introduce the I-System.

Fixers and depressors are attempts to prop up our sense of self by supporting the belief that we are damaged. Fixers are the ego suggesting solutions to the problem of why we're unhappy ("If I lost weight, I'd be more confident, and then I'd be able to find love") while depressors present the problem as overwhelming ("I'll never find love; I should just give up hoping for it"). This is not to suggest that there are no external factors that influence our lives—to suggest we have complete control over what happens to us is just as wrong as thinking we are damaged and need fixing. The point is that whether or not you lose weight, whether or not you find a partner, you are still *not* inherently damaged, and nothing external to you—losing weight, finding love, getting a raise, or winning a Nobel Prize—will create lasting happiness. We are the only ones who can do that for ourselves, and the only way it can be done is by accepting the inherently impermanent and empty nature of everything, including ourselves.

In a very general way, fixers can be related to anxiety (physically, fixers are associated with body tension, restlessness, or fast breathing) while depressors can be related to depression (and are associated with feeling heavy, tired, or pressured). Fixers create a sense of urgency; depressors engender a sense of helplessness. But despite these superficial differences, fixers and depressors are the exact same mechanism. They both function as explanations for why we are unhappy, and both reinforce the idea that unhappiness is something that can only be changed by outside factors becoming different— getting something we think we need or getting rid of something we dislike or fear. And while fixers seem to support the idea of a flexible self (in that they suggest that change is necessary for happiness), the suggested change, from a Zen perspective, is always superficial. Even major life changes, like getting a divorce or starting a new career, are superficial compared to the realization that the self is not actually real! Depressors are more obviously connected to the desire to see the self as permanent. Thoughts such as "Things will never change" and "I'll never get better/find love/get in shape" make us sad, but they are also reassuring. They tell us that the "I" really exists, exists so solidly, in fact, that it might as well be carved out of granite.[10]

One of my senior students gave a talk in which he noted that when we get a raise or get over being sick, or when spring arrives after a long winter, we are grateful for impermanence; so long as impermanence benefits us, we see the change as "good" and "deserved." It's only when things change in a way we don't like that we reject impermanence. His point is that we need to recognize that we all already embrace impermanence to some extent. This is absolutely true, and recognizing it can help make the idea of impermanence less scary. But I contend that when it comes to the impermanence of the self, *all* change is scary. Getting a raise is great, but it comes with a twinge of fear about earning this new salary. And while most sickness doesn't last long enough to become part of someone's identity, people with chronic illness do report being unable to enjoy days when they are free of pain or weakness because they're so busy worrying about when the pain and weakness will come back. Most people would rather accept that they will always be alone or miserable or broken in some way than confront head on the idea that the self is simply a collection of memories and actions, without any fixed ground. Otherwise, depressors would not work.

I introduced the idea of fixers in the last chapter because many times we focus on what we need to change in order to do better. But fixers and depressors can also be externally focused. The following map allows you to see what you think you need from others in order to be happy. Get a sheet of paper, and draw an oval like the one below, with this question inside: "What do I need from others to be happy?" Around the oval, write whatever thoughts come to you for the next three to four minutes. Don't censor yourself or evaluate what comes to mind—just write.

Once you're finished, it's time to review your answers and your reactions to writing them.

BODY TENSION
Is your body tense or relaxed?
Where is the tension being held?
Is your mind cluttered or clear?
What are your requirements?

Are there certain responses that cause significantly more tension than others? Sometimes it can be useful to do a spin-off map on specific responses that strongly activate your Identity-System. If you think this might be useful here or with any of these maps, just draw an oval, write the answer that created the most tension in the center, and repeat the mapping exercise with the new prompt.

Review the five omnipresent factors (invested contact, aversive or attractive reaction, getting hooked into patterns, self-motivated intentionality, invested attention). Take one of your answers and think about how that need evolves through the factors. For example, imagine you wrote, "I need love." Love is a wonderful thing, and I'm not suggesting you go without it! But to frame it as "I *need* love in order to be happy" can lead to problems as you work through the cycle of the factors. First, you grasp at the idea of love or the first sign of love in someone. The suggestion that someone loves you is so attractive that you immediately get hooked into a preexisting pattern of committing to that person before you actually know them. The idea that this person loves you becomes more important than the person, and finally you interpret everything they do as proof they love you or are falling out of love with you. You no longer see the person clearly; you only see what you think they can offer you. You no longer hold the relationship lightly; instead, you are constantly thinking about what you need to do to keep this person's love.

In the last chapter, I described how we instruct visitors to Soji to avoid adjusting their posture or scratching their nose, in order to confront the almost constant need to change conditions and thereby see our inability to simply be with what is. We think we can only be content if the world in general, or at least the people close to us, behave in certain ways or see us in a specific light. But is this really true? In chapter 2 we looked closely at the factors to understand how we move from contact with something or someone to investing that something or someone with the power to make us happy or miserable.

A way to make our attachment to external fixers and

depressors very apparent is to do a map that asks you to imagine giving them up. If you're interested in this exercise, draw an oval and in the center write, "What would happen if I gave up expecting X to make me happy?" The first couple of times you do this map, choose one of the specific answers you gave to the "What do I need from others to be happy?" map. After you've gotten used to exploring your reactions to specific fixers and depressors, you can try a more general formulation: "What would happen if I gave up expecting others to make me happy?" I don't recommend starting here, because this concept can be abstract enough that your ego might not feel threatened. But if you start with something quite particular—"What would happen if I gave up expecting my partner to make me happy?" or "What would happen if I gave up expecting money to make me happy?"—and pay attention to the physical and mental reactions, I think you'll find the reaction you have to be quite strong.

Look again at your "What do I need from others to be happy?" map and consider the body tension and the way you phrased what you wrote. Do you mainly focus on fixers or on depressors? Both lead to the same place, but it's useful to understand if you are anxiously trying to make your life better or sadly assuming the worst. You might also find that whether you are drawn to fixers or depressors can relate to which realm you are most drawn to: the god and demigod realms tend to go with fixers while the hungry ghost and hell realms are often built out of depressors.

Now do this map again with bridging. While writing, concentrate on the pressure of your body in the chair, the sound of a fan or air conditioner humming in the background, or the feeling of the pen or pencil as you write.

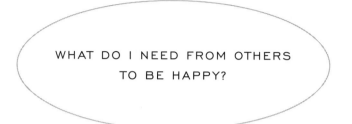

WHAT DO I NEED FROM OTHERS
TO BE HAPPY?

Do you find you have less body tension and mind clutter when you do this map with bridging? Do the fixers and depressors feel less vital compared to the first time you did the map? I hope so. The more we understand that we are not damaged in the present moment, the easier it is to see the pattern the omnipresent factors create over and over again.

Example: Ben is unhappy at his job, but every time a friend suggests he look for a new position, Ben shuts down. He feels convinced that no job would make him happy, so why bother changing? Ben does a map with the prompt "What do I need from others to be happy?" Here is the result:

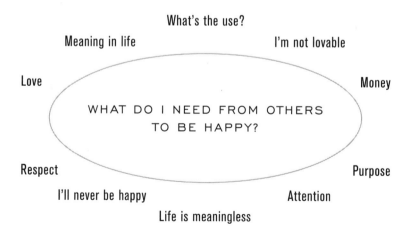

Looking at his answers, it becomes obvious to Ben that he uses depressors to support his sense that things are not going to get better. The thoughts that pop into his head, such as "Life is meaningless" and "I'll never be happy," are upsetting in one way but reassuring in another, because they make the world seem very predictable and stable. Ben realizes that it is not just his job that makes him unhappy, although that is the thing he focuses on. Instead, he has a strong pattern of selective viewing (the fifth factor)—he sees only the worst in any given situation because that both shores up his beliefs about the world (and himself) and excuses him from making any changes. After all, if every job is going to make him miserable, why go through the effort of job hunting? Ben sits with the feeling of hopelessness for a few weeks, practicing letting go of the idea that "this is how the world really is" over and over and does his map with bridging every few days. Gradually he loosens his grip on his belief that he is destined to be miserable forever. Next, Ben sits for thirty minutes every morning, lightly holding the intention to loosen his reliance on a worldview dictated by depressors.

Because so much of our sense of self is tied up in the external world and how we react to it, it can be useful to try different approaches to this question. If "What do I need from others to be happy?" doesn't resonate, you might instead do a map using the phrase "How my world should be." This map evokes the requirements in a very straightforward way, which makes spotting the fixers and depressors easier. For example, if one of your answers is "I should have an interesting job that pays well," your next thought might well be "But of course that will never happen" or "and I'm going to keep looking until I find that job!" Depressor or fixer, the point is that when you uncover your requirements, you uncover what you think you need in order to be happy.

Underlying the skandhas and the omnipresent factors are the twelve links in the chain of dependent origination. As we discussed in chapter 3, this is Buddhism's most basic and yet most detailed understanding of how suffering arises. It is like the I-System story line, which is when our Identity-System spins negative thoughts or requirements into a full-fledged story about our life and/or identity. Say you get turned down for a date. The requirement might be "People should give me a chance," and the depressor might be "I'll never find love." The story line takes this one step further—"I'm inherently unlovable." Now it becomes not just something that happens to you, but *who you are*. In the same way, dependent origination traces the path from the first moment of ignorance through the arising of craving and clinging, to the development of the self-identity based on that clinging. A lot of circumstantial things have changed between ancient India and the contemporary United States, but the basic human impulse to protect the self through stories remains the same.

An important map for exploring story lines is "How did I get to be the way I am?" As mentioned in chapter 5, this map can be general, or you can focus it on a specific issue. "How did I get to be an addict?" or "How did I get so far in debt?" The first time through, do the general map and see if you can uncover the story line that feels most important to your sense of identity.[11]

As before, write your thoughts as they come up, without censoring yourself. Don't limit yourself to obvious life-changing moments; if a small incident pops into your mind, put it down. It might stand for a type of event, or it might have a significance you didn't realize. You can focus on events— "I failed out of college" or "Working summers at the farm." Or on relationships—"My parents were very supportive." Or on feelings—"I was always ashamed of my weight." What matters is that you put down anything that feels like it shaped who you are right now. Finally, don't feel you should only put down negative responses. First, no one becomes who they are only because of negative experiences. Second, this can be a sneaky way the ego protects itself—dividing experiences as "good" and "bad" and cheerfully allowing the bad experiences to be rejected or dropped as a distraction from the fact that the ego is still clinging tightly to the good ones.

HOW DID I GET TO BE THE WAY I AM?

Once you're finished, it's time to review your answers and your reactions to writing them.

BODY TENSION
Is your body tense or relaxed?
Where is the tension being held?
Is your mind cluttered or clear?
What are your requirements?

See if you can determine a pattern in your answers—is there an overall story line that pulls together most or all of your responses? If not, don't worry that you've done the exercise wrong. (You haven't.) While many people have one dominant story line, other people have competing story lines or different story lines for different parts of their identity. You might find that if you do a map for "How did I get to be the parent (or child or partner) that I am?" you will have a very different set of responses from "How did I get to be the worker I am?" or "How did I get to be the hypochondriac that I am?" What is important here is not finding the one master or foundational story line (itself an attempt to impose order and permanence) but instead recognizing that story lines are not true. Even if a pattern does repeat ("I really do always pick partners who are bad for me"), that doesn't mean the pattern is fixed or intrinsic to who you are. It means that your consciousness is working very hard to make the patterns happen to create what is most important—the illusion of a coherent, stable, separate self.

When you do this map with bridging, you may find it hard to stay focused on the present moment, or you may feel a great deal of resistance. This is because story lines, like the twelve links, are very tightly tied to our sense of self. Therefore, uncovering and letting go of these stories can feel very threatening. Of course, if you don't find bridging hard, that's not a problem! Either way, just keep bringing your attention back to the present moment and your embodied sensations.

HOW DID I GET TO BE THE WAY I AM?

In the next chapter, we'll look at emotional states, as represented by the six realms, and we'll explore how individual maps help us determine the limits and requirements of those emotional states. Here requirements, fixers, depressors, and story lines will all come into play, as a whole system.

8

MIND MAPS AND REALMS

||||||||||||||||||||||||||||||||||||||||||||||||||||||||||||||||||||||||||||||||||||||||||||||||||||||||||||||||||||||||||||||

As NOTED IN chapter 4, the teaching of the six realms can be viewed in two ways. In traditional Buddhist cosmology, the realms were commonly understood as actual levels of existence through which beings passed across many rebirths. In this chapter, however, I'll be taking a more contemporary and psychological approach, considering the realms as emotional attitudes toward ourselves and our surroundings. These emotional attitudes are reinforced by conceptual rationalizations—we create stories to explain and justify our reactions to ourselves.[12] But these stories are generally false (if not completely false, then partially so), locating the source of our greed, anger, and delusion outside ourselves so that our reactions are not our fault.

The realms represent the various ways we suffer. The following maps will help you explore the psychological states and feelings that are represented by the six realms.

As I said before, although we all move in and out of all the realms, there is usually one realm (sometimes two) that we each favor and spend a lot of time in. It's useful to be able to recognize your "home realm." If your first reaction to any obstacle is anger, for example, you might want to focus on understanding and working with the hell realm. If the focus of your life has been comfort—for instance, you spend a lot of time in front of the TV or surfing the web—you might want to do god realm maps. Once you identify a home realm, I urge you to return to those maps regularly, rather than wait for an event or emotion connected to a realm to arise, because we tend to see our natural state or home realm as "normal" and not really something to explore. In truth, the exact opposite is true—what we consider to be our normal state of being or our usual reaction is actually the arena where our self is hardest at work, successfully creating the illusion of permanence.

THE GOD REALM

The first map is to help you see that, although the god realm seems like paradise, it is as much an ego prison as any other realm. This is not to say that wanting beautiful things is inherently bad, just that relying on having these things for happiness and a sense of self inevitably leads to unhappiness.

Take a blank piece of paper, and draw an oval with the question "What good or beautiful things do I wish for?" For several minutes, jot down around the oval your wishes for good, beautiful things or events. Perhaps it's a place filled with beautiful, splendid things, maybe a new car or house. Or it might be a desire for peace in the world and safety for everyone. List all the things you can think of, without pausing or censoring yourself.

> ## WHAT GOOD OR BEAUTIFUL THINGS
> ## DO I WISH FOR?

Once you're finished, it's time to review your answers and your reactions to writing them.

BODY TENSION
Is your body tense or relaxed?
Where is the tension being held?
Is your mind cluttered or clear?
What are your requirements?

Next, ask yourself why you want these things. If you believe they will make you feel happier or more peaceful, interrogate this belief. Even things like world peace are still external to yourself, and depending on something external for happiness is doomed to fail.

The second map more directly addresses the negative side of the god realm—addiction. As you do this map, think about addiction in the broadest sense—not just a physical dependency on drugs or alcohol but also addiction to the things, behaviors, and people you turn to automatically to relieve stress and block anxiety. Watching TV, eating junk food, having sex, and even thrill seeking can all be ways to avoid confronting reality.

As above, for three to four minutes jot down anything that

comes to mind. It's especially important that you don't censor yourself here; even if something comes up that seems unrelated, put it down.

WHAT AM I ADDICTED TO?

BODY TENSION
Is your body tense or relaxed?
Where is the tension being held?
Is your mind cluttered or clear?
What are your requirements?

Here it's especially important to review your body tension because "addiction" is a very loaded word and it's easy to throw up rationalizations and excuses as protection. Which answers make you feel most tense? Where and how does the tension manifest? If you don't feel tense, think about giving up each item on the list forever and see if the tension increases.

THE DEMIGOD REALM

Around the oval, describe all the behaviors you engage in to defend and maintain your happiness.

HOW DO I DEFEND MY HAPPINESS?

BODY TENSION
Is your body tense or relaxed?
Where is the tension being held?
Is your mind cluttered or clear?
What are your requirements?

The demigod realm is a realm of constant fighting, based in jealousy and fear of losing things, people, and identity. One of the first things we learn from Zen practice is that clinging leads to suffering, but that doesn't stop us from clinging. Sometimes we don't even recognize that we are clinging—we believe we are simply defending perfectly reasonable boundaries. Do you refuse to learn anything that is presented by outsiders? If yes, why?

Another map that you can do if you feel you are in the demigod realm is a jealousy map.

WHAT OR WHO AM I JEALOUS OF?

BODY TENSION
Is your body tense or relaxed?
Where is the tension being held?
Is your mind cluttered or clear?
What are your requirements?

Consider how this map made you feel in your body, not just in your mind. When we think about things or people that make us jealous, it is inevitable that we will tense up. Why? What is the story line here? Thoughts such as "I'm not enough" or "I'm always going to be abandoned" are what underlie jealousy and make people feel they have to defend or fight to keep what they have. But do you really have to feel this way? What would happen if you were enough, just by yourself, and people and things that make you happy could come and go without upsetting your core stability? The next step is to drop these ideas. As you sit in zazen, let go of any thoughts that come up about not being enough. Don't dwell on or inspect these thoughts (as you might when doing the maps), just drop them, over and over.

THE HUMAN REALM

For this map, identify specific goals you dwell on (whether or not you achieve them)—such as losing weight, getting out of debt, or being nicer to your family.

WHAT SPECIFIC GOALS
DO I DWELL ON?

BODY TENSION
Is your body tense or relaxed?
Where is the tension being held?
Is your mind cluttered or clear?
What are your requirements?

How do you act when you fall short of achieving or maintaining these goals? Especially consider why you hang on to goals that you continually fail at or that seem important in the abstract but that you never get around to putting energy into. What story do you tell yourself about why you need to achieve certain goals in order to be happy?

One of the great beliefs of the modern era is that we should be continually striving to improve ourselves. There's a whole self-help industry that tells us how to set goals and achieve them. Working toward a goal is not necessarily bad. But why do you want to improve your life? Is it because you really believe the idea that you're damaged and need to be fixed? Or that if you just achieve X, you'll finally be at peace with yourself?

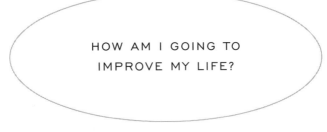

HOW AM I GOING TO
IMPROVE MY LIFE?

BODY TENSION
Is your body tense or relaxed?
Where is the tension being held?
Is your mind cluttered or clear?
What are your requirements?

As with goals, the seductive appeal of "improvement" is that we will be happier, better, and more complete if we can just improve that one thing about ourselves. I find this map to be one that often leads to a lot of mental clutter, so pay special attention to the third question.

THE ANIMAL REALM

The animal realm is the realm of fear and sensuality, which means it is also the realm of seeking creature comforts and favoring the familiar as a way to feel secure. Do you stick to what is familiar, even when it isn't offering you happiness, because of fear? This map asks you to think about what you are afraid of.

WHAT AM I AFRAID OF?

BODY TENSION
Is your body tense or relaxed?
Where is the tension being held?
Is your mind cluttered or clear?
What are your requirements?

Review the fears you have, and pick one or two that are most powerful. Do a map just around one of the fears. How do these fears drive you toward behaviors that are unskillful or even inappropriate?

THE HUNGRY GHOST REALM

Jot down around the oval things that you continually hunger for: entertainment, intellectual or spiritual achievement, sensual pleasure, or whatever they might be. Note: this map is different than the first (god realm) map in that it asks you to think about things you crave rather than wish for. Instead of thinking about things you would like to have, think about things that you can't get enough of or feel empty without. Remember not to censor yourself.

WHAT DO I CONTINUALLY HUNGER FOR?

BODY TENSION
Is your body tense or relaxed?
Where is the tension being held?
Is your mind cluttered or clear?
What are your requirements?

Which things cause the most mental turmoil and body tension? Note especially anything you are ashamed of. Is there a craving you don't want to admit (either for the thing itself or the intensity of the craving)? What kinds of things/situations cause you to feel inadequate?

Another way to think about this realm is to ask not what you want but what you lack. If thinking about what you lack is more powerful than thinking about what you want, go with the following map:

WHY AM I DISSATIFIED WITH MY LIFE?

BODY TENSION
Is your body tense or relaxed?
Where is the tension being held?
Is your mind cluttered or clear?
What are your requirements?

THE HELL REALM

This map is different than the others—instead of scattering thoughts around an oval, identify situations that trigger your aggression and anger. Then list the requirements for each trigger. Remember requirements are "should" statements— you aren't listing the things that cause the trigger but the beliefs you hold that cause the trigger to seem rational. For example, a trigger could be getting cut off while driving. The requirement would be something like, "Everyone should drive safely and respectfully."

This map is set up this way because the hell realm can only be created through a relationship to the outside world. The other realms are internal, even when they are focused on outward things. For instance, you can crave chocolate even while there is none in front of you. The hell realm, by contrast, is always external—you become angry in response to a perceived or real threat. So what makes you angry? A trigger, in this case, is anything that sets off the anger response, whether or not you feel the response is justified. Some examples of triggers are someone at work taking your lunch, being cut off in traffic, or your partner not listening to you. Once you identify the trigger, you should be able to identify the requirements that underlie the anger. Often there is more than one. "My partner should listen to me" is an obvious requirement, but you might also realize that "My partner should care about what I'm saying" and "My partner should always put my needs first" are also requirements that cause you to react with anger.

TRIGGERS	BODY TENSION	REQUIREMENTS
That person cut me off in traffic	*Pressure behind the eyes and top of head, shallow breathing*	*That person should drive more carefully*

Review your triggers first. Pick a couple that are most intense mentally and cause the strongest body tension. Consider how skillful your level of anger or aggression is. Notice I'm not asking you if your anger is justified or right. In Buddhism, we focus on skillful and unskillful means. Perhaps your anger makes you feel powerful for a moment, but what about after that? Does your anger lead to a better outcome the next time you are triggered, or do you just get angry again?

Next, consider your requirements. What do they tell you about your expectations of the world? You already know that the world is not going to arrange itself exactly the way you want it, so why keep insisting it do so? Underlying anger, especially anger that expresses itself in aggression, is usually equated with fear. Anger feels better than fear—more power-ful and therefore more secure. But being angry is picking up a hot coal to throw at someone—you get burned first. If you are able to let go of your anger, you can confront your fear and let go of that as well.

BRIDGING

You may have noticed that thus far in this chapter, I have not included any bridging maps. There's a reason for this. Since what we're talking about is emotional attitudes, one bridging map is enough, because what you will be focusing on is letting go of the feeling, not the specific situation. In other words, you don't want to do a map specifically about bridging what makes you jealous; instead, do bridging about the feeling (jealousy) itself. As you bridge, try to let go of the feelings of jealousy (or anger or craving) rather than letting go of your jealousy *about* your partner or letting go of your craving *for* alcohol. Through this one map, you can see how bridging can be used to address all the realms.

Consider the emotional state most closely identified with the map you did. If there is more than one emotion connect-ed to the realm, try to be specific about which one dominat-ed your map. So, for example, if two people do the demigod map "How do I defend my happiness?" one person might feel that anxiety was the most powerful emotion that came up during the map, while the other person might find the question rouses a great deal of anger. Whatever the emotion, take a moment to really tune in to the embodied sensations of the present moment—the background noise or the feel-ing of your body in the chair. Then write anything that comes up when you think about the emotion, but without getting pulled away from that focus. See if you can prove to yourself that in this exact moment, you are not afraid or jealous or numb.

BRIDGING MAP

Write the emotion you feel in the oval. Before you start writing, listen to background sounds and feel your body's pressure on your seat, your feet on the floor, and the pen in your hand. Take your time. Once you are settled, keep feeling the pen in your hand as you start writing. Watch the ink go onto the paper and listen to background sounds. For the next few minutes, jot down any thoughts that come to mind.

How does your body act in this state
(when feeling jealousy, anger, etc.)?

Is your I-System on or off?
If it's on, rate the intensity of your I-System from 1–10.
If your I-System is active, repeat the exercise until the I-System turns off.

As we finish this chapter, I want to remind you that mind maps and bridging are not the end goal. Bridging leads to the engagement of your Executive Function (the opposite of the Identity-System), where you operate out of a sense of wholeness. But in Zen terms, bridging doesn't promote intimacy with your problems because there's still a split focus—you're thinking about bad thoughts but focusing on background sounds and so forth. In positive samadhi, you drop the idea of subject and object and thus create the intimacy that will allow you, paradoxically, to stop clinging to the problem.

And even positive samadhi should not be equated with zazen. In zazen, you are dropping all thoughts and letting go of everything, even internal concentration and focus. This is the third step in the path of freedom from suffering. Maps uncover self-imposed limitations. Bridging helps you see that the limitations are not actually in the present moment. Samadhi allows you to become so intimate with the supposed limits that you recognize they are not limits at all. And zazen, practiced regularly, leads to dropping off body and mind and thus dropping the notion that we have a stable, unchanging self that needs protecting. This is freedom.

9

MAPS FOR ZEN

IN THIS CHAPTER, we'll explore mind maps intended to help people overcome resistance to or obstacles in their practice. The most common forms of resistance are distraction, boredom, and anxiety. Distraction is what happens when you sit down on your cushion, but instead of following your breath or letting go of what comes up, you replay an argument, plan your day, or imagine your next vacation. Slipping into thinking happens all the time, but if you find yourself distracted from start to finish or deliberately using meditation time to think about other things, you are resisting the practice. Boredom with practice often presents as a general lack of interest in sitting, but it can also have a feeling of frustration—that there's no point or this isn't working. Anxiety is when you find yourself worried that you are "wasting" time "just sitting here" and fretting over the need to get up and get stuff done. Underneath all of these forms of resistance is fear—the fear that a moment of clarity will make it impossible to go back to the comfortable and familiar way of thinking.

FINDING A TEACHER

I want to stress (again) that the absolute best way to deepen your practice is to work regularly with a teacher. Zen, at its heart, is about the lived experience of the present moment, and the interaction of teacher and student in that present moment is one of its most powerful mechanisms. Reading books or listening to taped dharma talks can actually reinforce avoidance to working with a teacher. Studying on our own can make us believe that we have achieved a deep understanding and therefore we don't need a teacher. This in turn allows us to avoid surrender and defend our belief in our independence. In addition, we humans are brilliant at telling ourselves what we want to hear; it's all too easy to read a teaching or listen to a talk and interpret it to reinforce what we already believe! Finally, the lack of the physical presence of the teacher and sangha makes it harder to connect to the power of the dharma.

If you can, find a teacher, and work with him or her, even if doing so is inconvenient. Remember that Dōgen, the founder of Soto Zen, traveled from Japan to China, mostly on foot, to find a teacher! I have been a spiritual seeker all my life, and at different times I've gone to great lengths to practice with a teacher. Before I encountered Zen, I traveled to India to meet with the Sikh spiritual teacher Kirpal Singh, who died nineteen days after I arrived. For a period in my forties, every week I would drive a hundred miles round trip from my job in Albany for study group and sitting at Mount Tremper. Later on, I left a well-paying job and moved from New York to Utah to study with Genpo Roshi. If you truly want to pursue practice, make it the center of your life. This doesn't mean giving up your job or relationships or becoming a monk; it does mean making practice a priority, not a hobby.

Real practice involves a complete reorientation of one's life in such a way that one's activities are manifestations of and are filled with a deeper meaning. For this to happen, practice must be the dominant concern in our lives. All other considerations must be subordinated. Thus, we make a shift; we turn away from ordinary things to practice as the most important thing in our lives. When I say we turn away from ordinary activities, I don't mean a literal cessation but rather a change in attitude toward them. Turning away reflects a reorientation of values. Instead of seeking ultimate fulfillment in pleasure, power, wealth, or a fine reputation, we see the dharma as having the greatest value and the greatest potential for fulfillment.

"What Is Practice? Arousing the Thought of Enlightenment," 2015

One more word about teachers—make sure you have a real connection to your teacher. As noted in the preface, when I went to a weekend retreat in Vermont and met Maezumi Roshi there, I felt I had come home. Working with Maezumi was an intense experience. Interview was a practice in surrender because he could see right through his students. I learned to drop my guard and open to him, a true meeting of the minds. You should feel the same respect for and trust in your teacher, and if that connection isn't there, you need to seek elsewhere.

Hopefully you'll feel a connection with your teacher, immediately or soon after meeting them. Over time this develops into a trust; if a teacher demands commitment or loyalty right away, this is something to be cautious of. Sometimes, especially with a charismatic teacher, you'll want to believe everything the teacher says right away, but don't let go of your common sense! And if a teacher breaks your trust, consider how they react when you confront them. Someone who insists it is a teaching and refuses to apologize is more concerned with their reputation than the dharma.

Having said all that, it may seem hypocritical for me to suggest using mind maps to help your practice, but I'm aware that for many people, no level of dedication will make a weekly meeting with a teacher possible. These mind maps have a great advantage over reading or listening to talks, which is that they are interactive. They get your resistance and ideas out of your head, separated from you, so you can examine them with some dispassion and clarity. So if you cannot find a teacher or can only see your teacher once a month or less, you may find these maps helpful if you are feeling stuck or resistant. They also can be very useful for practitioners who find their practice plateauing—perhaps a sense of being in the "doldrums" in zazen or noticing that no amount of meditation seems to be changing habitual behaviors that lead to suffering. Keep in mind that the maps are only the first step. After you have uncovered the problem or resistance, you need to take the next step to achieving positive samadhi; that is, you need to move from bridging about the problem to being intimate with it, if only briefly, without the act of writing and thus without making a clear subject and object. Sink into the problem and focus on it until you really understand its contours and weight. Then, when you do zazen, let even that understanding go—drop both your understanding of the problem and the problem itself. Drop everything and just be present.

MIND MAPS FOR ZEN

The first map is a variation on the map "Who am I?" This map takes the question and gives it a Zen emphasis, asking you to focus intently on what's going on *right now*. All mind maps ask you to scatter thoughts quickly and without censoring yourself, but with this map it is especially important. If you can't think of anything, just write "blank" and keep going until time runs out. Don't let yourself stray into the future or the past, hopes or regrets.

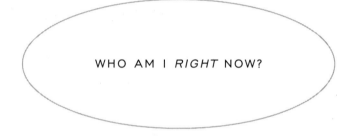

WHO AM I *RIGHT* NOW?

BODY TENSION
Is your body tense or relaxed?
Where is the tension being held?
Is your mind cluttered or clear?
What are your requirements?

You may find that you have less tension and mental clutter when you think about who you are in this very moment. This is useful information to have—you know that if you are able to stay in the present moment, you will be at ease in more of your life. On the other hand, some people freeze up when asked to identify who they are in this very moment. This may seem like the opposite reaction to feeling relaxed, but it is coming from the same place—an instinctive realization that in the present moment there is no fixed identity. This freezing, however, is a form of resistance. The hesitation is a desire to keep a sense of separation between the self and the present.

Now consider the story line this map has produced and recognize that right here, right now, any story line is wrong. In this very instant, you are not a professional or a student, a wife or a daughter, a marathon runner or a knitter. At this moment, you just *are*. Think about what it would be like to simply be, to interact with whatever is happening without story lines or baggage. Don't forget, with this or any map in this chapter, to redo the map with bridging. It's especially important when you are doing a map about your practice to bring yourself into your body, into the present moment, and become aware of how that reduces anxiety, mind clutter, and body tension.

Imagining yourself existing in the eternal present can be unsettling, even frightening. The next map can help you understand what you fear (or hope for) in practice. It can be very useful if you are frustrated with how your practice is going.

HOW AM I GOING TO
IMPROVE MY LIFE?

BODY TENSION
Is your body tense or relaxed?
Where is the tension being held?

Is your mind cluttered or clear?
What are your requirements?

When I've used this map in my study group, I've found that some students produce a completely blissful map—no worries or struggles ever again. Other students produce an almost apocalyptic vision of themselves—hopeless and isolated because nothing is real. The first approach is actually a fixer—people who respond this way are covering over and defending their fears, especially the fear of nonexistence. This is a form of spiritual bypassing, and if you encounter it in yourself, I'd like to suggest you dig deeper. The second approach sees embracing impermanence only in terms of what has to be given up and how much that loss will hurt. It's easy to see that in this reaction a depressor is talking; compared to the fixer reaction, the depressor defense is more obviously related to fears. What the map demonstrates is not the path itself but what is holding us back from the path—either unrealistic expectations that lead to frustration or unexpressed fears of loss that lead to resistance. This particular map is a very good map to do with bridging, whereby you can experience the question neutrally, without being either blissed out or terrified. The bridging activates the Executive Function and short-circuits the fears and worries about the permanence of the self. Thus, we can encounter the idea of embracing impermanence without setting the Identity-System on high alert. Let me remind you that bridging involves redoing the map while tuning in to background sounds or sensations. When you move to zazen, you are dropping everything, not only the map and the background sensations but the question itself.

The next two maps are a pair that allows you to bring out

fears concerning a very common problem in Zen practice. As Zen students, we vow to save all sentient beings and strive to meet everyone with openness and compassion. This is based on the deep realization that, on an absolute level, there is no "you" or "me" because we are all one. But often that realization takes a while to manifest or is clear only intellectually and not in a real, embodied sense. On a relative level, being open to everyone is scary and even feels dangerous: What if someone takes advantage of me? Do I really have to care about *everyone*? Does this mean I have to be a vegetarian? This conflict can lead to feeling like a Zen failure, which in turn can lead to giving up practice. And for those who don't give up completely, this fear often leads to practicing with conditions: "I don't need to care about everyone" or "I can have a complete connection with myself after I lose weight." To delve into this territory, I encourage students to explore the following mind map:

WHAT PREVENTS ME FROM ESTABLISHING A FULLER CONNECTION WITH MYSELF?

BODY TENSION
Is your body tense or relaxed?
Where is the tension being held?
Is your mind cluttered or clear?
What are your requirements?

This map can often create strong feelings and is a good one to do on a regular basis—maybe once a month or even once a week.

The next map explores the same question in terms of your connections to others. If you feel that you just can't be open and compassionate with a certain person or group, feel free to substitute that specific name for the more general "others" in the prompt and see what comes up.

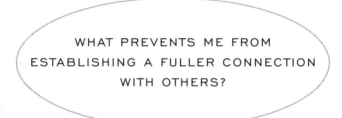

WHAT PREVENTS ME FROM ESTABLISHING A FULLER CONNECTION WITH OTHERS?

BODY TENSION
Is your body tense or relaxed?
Where is the tension being held?
Is your mind cluttered or clear?
What are your requirements?

This map shows the power others have over our sense of value and identity, leading us to present a partial and often carefully curated version of ourselves. If we have no story line or requirements, we can be completely open to and fully connected to others. Just as the previous map can reveal fears we have about what we have to give up to be Zen students, this map can reveal what holds us back from seeking a sangha.

The next map is a challenging one and requires a bit of explanation. Shunryū Suzuki Roshi, the founder of the San

Francisco Zen Center, once said that we become discouraged in our practice when we are being greedy with it. What he meant was when we sit with expectations in order to get something, we are going to become frustrated. As I tell my students, it's called "realization" not "getization" because there is nothing to get. It's very hard to let go of all our desires around practice, especially if we are practicing regularly and putting significant time into it. If you find yourself feeling frustrated, feeling that you aren't getting anywhere, consider doing the following map:

WHAT DO I THINK I SHOULD
GET FROM MY PRACTICE?

BODY TENSION
Is your body tense or relaxed?
Where is the tension being held?
Is your mind cluttered or clear?
What are your requirements?

Ask yourself how your greed for results, your desire for an enlightenment experience, or your hope to become a better, nicer, calmer person can lead to frustration and hinder your practice. Look at all the things you've written around the oval and ask yourself, "If I knew I would never get any of these, would I continue to practice?" If the answer is "No, I would not continue to practice," (and of course it almost always is) then realize that you are sitting with expectations, which is the exact thing that will hamper your progress. In this practice, to fail is to succeed. As hard as that is to accept, you must!

Finally, I'd like to offer two all-purpose maps. The first is very useful when you feel great resistance to actually sitting down and meditating. If you find yourself saying "I don't have time" or "I don't feel like it" day after day, consider doing the following map, and hopefully you'll be able to dig into what's really causing you to turn away from practice. As always, scatter your thoughts around the oval, but be very sure this time that you don't censor yourself, because the temptation to offer only "good" reasons for not practicing will be very strong.

WHAT'S STOPPING ME
FROM PRACTICING?

BODY TENSION
Is your body tense or relaxed?
Where is the tension being held?
Is your mind cluttered or clear?
What are your requirements?

The second map can help you keep your practice fresh, and, in some minor way, it can serve the function of a teacher—pointing out what you need to be doing now to make your practice rich and powerful. You might realize you need to go on a retreat (even for one day) or find a teacher (or visit your teacher more often). You might realize you need a community. Maybe you'll discover you need more than silent meditation—adding chanting or ritual may give you what you're missing. And sometimes the answer for all of us is simply that we need to stop daydreaming and actually meditate!

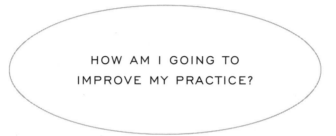

HOW AM I GOING TO
IMPROVE MY PRACTICE?

BODY TENSION
Is your body tense or relaxed?
Where is the tension being held?
Is your mind cluttered or clear?
What are your requirements?

10

THE SUTRAS
AND MIND MAPS

As I mentioned earlier, for some years now I have worked with my students to study the conjunction of Buddhist texts and mind maps. In addition to the Abhidharma, we have studied some of the key texts of Mahayana and Zen Buddhism, including the *Diamond Sutra*, the *Platform Sutra*, the *Vimalakirti Sutra*, and the *Lotus Sutra*. We have sought to understand the meaning of the sutras and to explore how the ideas of these texts relate to the modern world and our lives. Although, in this book, I cannot possibly reproduce the in-depth study the group has undertaken (we spent several *years* on the *Diamond Sutra*), I do want to share some of the mind maps that have gone along with the texts, as well as some key points about the sutras. I hope this taste encourages you to investigate these works more fully. Though most practitioners are comfortable reading the many, many works exploring Buddhism in modern terms (of which this book is one!), to many of us, the ancient texts seem too foreign to grapple with. They certainly are dense, and the cultural references and writing style are far from our own. But this does not mean that they are not worth the effort—quite the opposite! I believe that studying the original texts is second only to consistent zazen as a way to create the conditions for awakening. It is true that Zen prides itself on being beyond words and outside of scriptures. But you'll notice that in many stories of ancient Zen masters, they studied intently for years before reaching that place that is beyond words.

DIAMOND SUTRA

We have a printed copy of the *Diamond Sutra* dating from 868 C.E., which makes it the oldest complete printed book in existence. The care taken to preserve this text for over a thousand years (and the sutra itself is much older) points to its central importance. The title refers to the ability of a diamond to cut anything, and this sutra's wisdom cuts through all delusion. The amount of wisdom packed into this short text is incredible, but I want to focus on just one central and radical thread. The main point of the *Diamond Sutra* is that there is nothing to attain and no one to attain it. In successive chapters, the sutra urges readers to let go of attachment: attachment to acquiring merit, to the notion of a separate self, to the absolute, to emptiness, and even to the dharma itself. The line I quoted in the introduction—"Abiding no place, raise the Bodhi mind"—is the concentrated form of this idea: do not rest anywhere, take nothing as fixed or permanent, and then you will have the insight of a buddha.

The depths of nonattachment this work insists on are what make it so radical. Nothing is to be clung to, not even the dharma. The Buddha refers to his teachings as a raft that one uses to get to the other shore (that is, to attain enlightenment), and once you have achieved that, you have no need of the teachings, any more than you would carry the raft into the forest with you once you have crossed the river. Some people find this level of nonattachment to be frightening, even intellectually, and all Buddhists grapple with what this might mean on a day-to-day basis. How do we drop *everything* and still live in the world? Is it even possible to drop all attachments and clinging?

One way to begin to approach these questions is to bring up fears you might have that nonattachment means nonexistence. Here is a map—based in the question "Who am I?"—that we explored in the skandha chapter but framed in a more confrontational way. Read the prompt and then write your reactions to it around the outside of the oval.

I'M NOBODY.

BODY TENSION
Is your body tense or relaxed?
Where is the tension being held?
Is your mind cluttered or clear?
What are your requirements?

What was your first reaction? Was it anger at the perceived attack on your existence? Was it fear? Was it confusion? Earlier I mentioned that Zen students try to become "one true person of no rank," and I just quoted the idea of abiding no place, but somehow being "nobody" feels more personal, more of a threat. Take some time to consider what feels threatened and why.

If this map seems too radical, or you have trouble coming up with thoughts and ideas in response to "I'm nobody," here is another way to approach the idea of letting go of everything. For this map, instead of contemplating the idea that you are nobody, consider what you do to convince yourself that you are somebody.

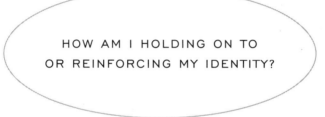

HOW AM I HOLDING ON TO
OR REINFORCING MY IDENTITY?

BODY TENSION
Is your body tense or relaxed?
Where is the tension being held?
Is your mind cluttered or clear?
What are your requirements?

Interestingly, when we feel abandoned, we have to recognize that we are rejecting the part of us that feels strong and independent. When we feel the need to cling to something or to prove we exist, we are rejecting our buddha-nature, which is vast and groundless and beyond words. Consider what you do to prove not only that you exist but that you matter. Consider why. It can be a very revealing study.

Even though these maps are connected to complicated

sutras, they are approached in the same way. When you do the map, take only three to four minutes to write your responses, but then, before you do a bridging map, remember to take time to center yourself, relax, and tune in to your chosen sound or sensation. If you have an interest in reading the sutra, once you have pinpointed your requirements, fixers, and story lines, you can return to the sutra and reread it, discovering deeper meanings. And even if you don't return to the sutra, keep your maps (I use a three-ring binder) so that you can look back over them and compare changes over time.

LOTUS SUTRA

Like the *Diamond Sutra,* the *Lotus Sutra* is considered one of the foundational texts of Mahayana Buddhism. Many consider it the Buddha's final teaching, which encompasses and surpasses all previous teachings. This sutra reconciles apparently contradictory teachings of the Buddha with the idea of "one teaching, many vehicles"—that is, the idea that the Buddha taught in different ways depending on the nature of his audience but that all teachings, rightly understood, point to the one vehicle, or the single great teaching. In the *Lotus Sutra,* that central teaching is revealed to be the truth that all beings (including women—a radical thought in ancient India!) can become buddhas, that all beings (even those who commit evil acts, such as murder) have buddha-nature.

Although this seems like a much more easily accepted and palatable idea than the *Diamond Sutra*'s demand for complete nonattachment, the idea that all beings have buddha-nature is equally challenging to practice. There are always groups or individuals we not only don't like but think we are completely justified for not liking. To think that child abusers or war criminals are buddhas just feels wrong. And on a personal level, it can be incredibly hard to believe that we should treat as a buddha, for example, that guy at work who rarely does anything useful but got a promotion because his uncle is friends with the boss. At the very least, we want to believe that all these people need to become aware of their crimes (or sins), repent, and even be punished. But that they have inherent buddha-nature while abusing children or bombing their own citizens or smugly believing they deserve the promotion? No way!

The *Lotus Sutra* uses parables and stories of mythical figures to explore the discomfort that this teaching provokes. Over and over, the Buddha's most advanced followers grapple with the problem of universal buddha-nature. In fact, early on, when the Buddha announces that he is going to share this final wisdom, five thousand of the gathered followers walk out, believing that they do not need the teaching. (Or were they just afraid of what it would show them about themselves?) Some of the parables are familiar, such as the one about a person whose friend sews a rich jewel into the hem of his garment only to suffer in poverty for years, not realizing the riches are right there.

One story that I find very powerful on a psychological level is the parable of a bodhisattva named Never Despise. This man respected everyone he met and said to everyone, "I dare not slight you, because you are all to become buddhas." While you would think this would be taken as a compliment, the people he met instead became angry and even beat him. Why is this? In psychology, there is a behavior pattern called projection. This is the practice of attributing to other people traits we find unappealing, despite that we ourselves either unconsciously manifest them or secretly fear we are guilty of them. It's a defense mechanism: we project onto others the traits we most dislike in ourselves. Although you may be familiar with this idea, it's probably not clear how it applies to the story of Never Despise. If I label as "projection" the behavior of the people who were insulting and beating him up, wouldn't that mean they unconsciously think they love and respect all beings? Why would anyone find that a reason for violence? There are two answers to this. First, those attacking Never Despise are attacking him for being stupid and naive, naive enough to believe everyone is good. Being cynical, they fear being tricked or manipulated, so they see Never Despise's respect of them as a weakness. But that is not all they are projecting.

As I've written many times in this book, the most important goal of the ego is to maintain the illusion that it exists—that the self is a coherent, permanent, and unique entity. And I've mentioned how some students will turn away from practice when they get a glimpse of the truth that there is no separate self. If you remember this, you can see why people might respond to Never Despise with anger. He is telling everyone that they have buddha-nature, that they will become buddhas. But to believe this one must accept the idea that the self is an illusion—we all have buddha-nature because we are all part of the One Body. What appears to be a separate self and a separate body is just a momentary manifestation, just as a wave only exists because it is part of the ocean. So the anger and hatred people feel toward the bodhisattva Never Despise is a defense mechanism, a way to avoid seeing the truth. They *do* unconsciously fear that they are buddhas, because to recognize that would mean recognizing that they are not intrinsically separate from everything else. Their hatred toward Never Despise suddenly makes sense.

Looking at smaller forms of projection that are driven by

the ego's fear of not having a unique self is a very useful practice, and often the better starting point than trying to let go of the ego all at once. Seeing one's projection is a simple way to dissolve boundaries. To reclaim some facet of the self that appears to be not-self is the first step toward letting go of the concept of the self completely. In other words, when we realize that a projection, which appears to exist "out there," external to the self, is really our own reflection, we have torn down that particular boundary between self and not-self. As an example, if the people who attacked Never Despise were willing to reclaim and accept their stupidity, it would make it easier for them to recognize their own buddha-nature because they would no longer feel the need to reject any part of themselves.

This kind of work is especially important regarding our shadow sides, the parts of ourselves we'd like to pretend don't exist. That kind of pretending in fact only makes our disgust toward the trait we dislike stronger. Instead of trying hard to separate, consider accepting those parts of yourself that you fear or hate, as a step on the path to seeing that all the parts of "yourself" are just the skandhas at work, maintaining the pretense of the permanent self.

The following map can help you move from the position of the people throwing things at the bodhisattva Never Despise to the position of being him. Think of someone you despise. I use that word deliberately—think of someone for whom your feeling is not only strong but carries with it a sense of disgust and moral superiority. We can hate someone and still respect them, but despising someone means having a level of contempt that is personal. That is because you are despising traits you worry about having yourself, so the feeling is literally personal.

Your first response to the prompt might be to say you don't

despise anyone. That's possible, but unlikely. It is more likely that you are protecting yourself by resisting what the map can reveal. But if you can't think of a specific person, try a group or a behavior.

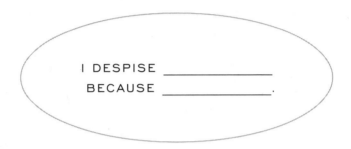

I DESPISE _____

BECAUSE _____.

BODY TENSION
Is your body tense or relaxed?
Where is the tension being held?
Is your mind cluttered or clear?
What are your requirements?

As you write, note where and how strong your body tension is. Often, this map causes very high levels of tension because it gets close to fears we have about ourselves. You may find one or two of the answers are powerful enough to need their own maps to explore. When you are finished, review your answers and ask yourself, "How is this me?" Do this as its own map. The answers can be very revealing. A student of mine created a short version of this map that can be done at any moment—whenever you have an angry or disgusted thought or reaction, say, "And that's me" to remind yourself of projection.

VIMALAKIRTI SUTRA

While this sutra is not as well known as the previous two, it is a wonderful text that deserves more attention. Like the *Lotus Sutra*, it stresses universal enlightenment—Vimalakirti is a married householder with a business, children, and servants. Yet his understanding of the dharma is advanced beyond all the monks and bodhisattvas who attend on the Buddha. He demonstrates the importance of carrying practice into everyday life and not creating false divisions between "practice" and "ordinary life" nor between "sacred" and "profane."

The sutra demonstrates how to abandon these dichotomies (and others) by completely understanding nonduality. The bodhisattvas in the assembly each attempt to explain nonduality. The last bodhisattva, Manjushri, says that by trying to give an answer, all the others have already fallen into dualism, and this seems to be the conclusion. But when they turn to Vimalakirti, he simply remains silent.

Of course, there is silence, and then there is silence. Only a very deep understanding of emptiness can express the truth of nonduality through silence. For the rest of us, words are still important as a path toward understanding because it is very difficult to drop off the thinking mind and truly *be*. Indeed, silence on (or not thinking about) topics can be the result of a shallow acceptance, either of your own unexamined beliefs or of cultural norms—the exact opposite of understanding nonduality.

To delve into this territory of approaching nondual silence, let's take an example rooted in our own culture. Consider the idea of God (or, if you prefer, a myth or archetype, like the hero or the mage). The ideas we have about God or archetypes are designed to help people negotiate the obscure regions of our psyche, the regions that are difficult to access directly but that profoundly influence our thoughts and behaviors. We create an idea of God because we want something tangible, something external to ourselves that explains what is confusing or problematic about the world.

Do a mind map where you list the things that come to mind when you think about God. Even if you're an atheist, if you're a person who grew up in Western culture, you have a conception of God. This map isn't about what you *believe*; it's about what you think of when you think of God.

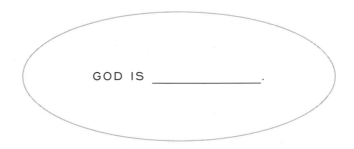

GOD IS _____.

BODY TENSION
Is your body tense or relaxed?
Where is the tension being held?
Is your mind cluttered or clear?
What are your requirements?

Consider the fact that every religion holds as true the concept of God's ineffable nature—God is beyond human understanding and beyond words. But do we really believe that? How much were you able to write down around the oval? How many of these thoughts and descriptions feel true? Whether you consider yourself a devout Christian or a strong atheist, the point is the same—we don't like things that are beyond our understanding. We may say we want to experience God or enlightenment, but mostly what we want to experience is the self we think we'll be if we have a transcendent moment. Only by peeling back the layers of beliefs and concepts can we get to the place where silence is the answer.

PLATFORM SUTRA

This work—the discourses of the Sixth Patriarch of Chinese Zen, Hui-Neng (638–713 C.E.)—is the only teaching not by the Buddha to be designated a sutra. In many ways, this is the most approachable of the sutras I have discussed. The focus of Hui-Neng's teachings is to understand true suchness, or life just as it is, with nothing added. Over and over again, he uses dichotomies to demolish dichotomies. There is no difference, for example, between sudden and gradual enlightenment, between existence and nonexistence, nor even between nirvana and *samsara* (the conditioned world of suffering). Samsara *is* nirvana.

The following map can help you see your own dichotomies, to see how you are hanging on to dualism. There are a lot of ways to respond to the prompt: "I'm not X enough," "I'm not enough for X," or even just your emotional response to the prompt. Don't censor yourself—write down anything that comes into your mind.

I'M NOT ENOUGH.

BODY TENSION
Is your body tense or relaxed?
Where is the tension being held?
Is your mind cluttered or clear?
What are your requirements?

The *Platform Sutra* transcends existence and nonexistence. This exercise shows that we have not yet accomplished such transcendence. We are attached to thoughts, to positive things, to our identity. We are also attached to the hope of getting rid of things about ourselves we don't like. We keep trying to fix ourselves. We suffer because we are attached to our concepts. Part of mindfulness, part of your practice, can be using mind map exercises such as this to see where you are stuck and what concepts keep you stuck.

This is a very brief overview of just four of the many Buddhist sutras and is in no way intended to be comprehensive. Rather, I hope this chapter has introduced you to the way sutra study can enrich both your practice and your life. Too often, Buddhism in the United States becomes synonymous with meditation or even just mindfulness. There are incredible riches in the sutras—hundreds of years of wisdom about and elaboration of the Buddha's teachings. Although zazen remains the heart of any Zen practice, I hope I have whetted your appetite to explore the primary texts and see how they apply to you.

11

COMMITMENT

THE PSYCHOLOGIST ROBERT Augustus Masters writes, "Spirituality—the cultivation of intimacy with what we, in our heart of hearts, know to be sacred or ultimate—cannot be left out of any serious consideration of what it means to be human."[13] In this book I have attempted to address the question of what it means to be human by drawing awareness to how we thwart our ability to live a fully human life.

The models we've explored from the Abhidharma and the I-System demonstrate the means by which we avoid the reality of our existence. While the two models aren't a perfect fit, they do point us in the right direction. They both take up the process of mental functioning and explore how our typical functioning hinders us from being free and at peace in the world and with ourselves. The Abhidharma approaches this issue from the transcendental, while the I-System does so from a modern understanding of psychology. Modern psychology is starting to recognize that ideas about humanity dating back thousands of years in Buddhist philosophy dovetail with its own findings.[14] Just as studies of the brain with MRIs have shown that the Buddha's description of consciousness parallels the scientific understanding of the mind, the Abhidharma turns out to foreshadow the way psychology understands the emotional and existential problems of human life.

I hope the mind maps I've shared are a helpful way to explore the things that hold you back: from practice, from escaping destructive patterns, from being at ease in your life. Before I close this book, I would like to discuss a topic I find of paramount importance regarding practice: commitment. "Commitment" is an easy word to say, and we all think we know what it means—to make a promise and stick to it, to continue on a path despite setbacks and distractions. But there is more to commitment—especially in Buddhist practice—than just consistency. The Abhidharma and the I-System aid in commitment to the path because they can uncover our resistance to coming face-to-face with the impermanent nature of the self and all that goes along with that realization.

To become enlightened is not about perfecting our relative state of being; it is about recognizing our true nature. Though in this book I have emphasized how strongly the ego strives to maintain the illusion that the self exists, it is important to realize that our buddha-nature is also striving to find (or, more accurately, regain) a deep connection to the One Body. We strive to be better than or different from others, but we also strive to make connections, and every time we sit down on the cushion, we are making a connection with the present moment and everything in it. We need to be consciously and actively committed to supporting our buddha-nature and being present for what is. This is how we take the practice off the cushion and also how we reduce the pressure of the ego.

It can be very scary to face the losses that dedicated practice will bring—the fact that what we lose has never truly been real does not make giving up the illusions any less wrenching. So we need commitment from the start to carry us through the wrenching moments. Without commitment there will be no genuine transformation because we will always be practicing with conditions. We'll always find a way to hold back a little bit of the self. We'll promise to save all sentient beings . . . except that group of really bad people. We'll strive to let go of all desires . . . except for the couple we think make us better. We'll try to be present for what is . . . unless we really don't like what is.

To practice without conditions is very hard; indeed, I don't think anyone ever fully lets go of all conditions, although we can all have moments when we let go. When we commit to the practice, we make a choice to face ourselves and become fully engaged in life. Commitment therefore requires a willingness to let go of the safety of what is familiar yet limiting. In fact, commitment actually brings a loss of freedom—the loss of the freedom to be not fully responsible, to pretend we don't know better. We lose superficial freedom to live in the midst of a more profound freedom.

This level and kind of commitment is frightening because it means committing to facing reality. We have mastered the art of taking refuge in things that provide an illusion of safety, ease, and happiness. But in taking refuge in the three treasures—the Buddha, dharma, and sangha—we vow to seek the path that leads to liberation and follow it to the end. When we take refuge in the three treasures, we recognize that things are not what we would like them to be—they are not reliable, solid, and safe. We also recognize that the ego does not have control over reality and that our desire for security just leads to more delusion as we try (and fail) to control our world. Commitment to the path requires relinquishing control, a kind of surrender, which is something the self fears. Remember that when we looked at the skandhas, we discovered that once consciousness is established, its first priority is to ensure its existence. Consciousness seeks to stabilize and protect the sense that it is permanent and separate from the rest of the world rather than impermanent and inextricably tied up in everything else. Recall that the links of dependent origination result in a constant rebirth or regeneration of our ego, which inevitably leads to decay and—assuming we're still attached—to suffering.

To commit to the path is to confront the ego with its own demise, and on some level, we know this. This is why commitment to Zen can be so disturbing. This is why, over the years, I have seen many people have a glimpse of realization, a moment of awakening . . . and then never seen them at the center again. Of course, people have various reasons for leaving, but I am always surprised at how often people abandon the practice just as they have or are clearly about to make a breakthrough. Commitment means letting go of what we hold to be unchallengeable, namely the ego's need for control. We must also leave behind our old habits and delusions. We must inhabit a state of emptiness, a place where nothing is fixed and where logic does not reach—a state in which our true nature can be revealed.

It's important to recognize that inhabiting this state of emptiness does not mean killing the ego. Without our ego, we wouldn't get out of bed in the morning! We want the ego to give up control, to serve as a first mate rather than as the captain. But too often we believe that the ego needs to be the center of everything in order to be healthy. This is not true; an ego is healthier when it doesn't have to work constantly to maintain its sense of importance. We all know people who always have to be the center of attention, who feel threatened as soon as they are not in the limelight. And we all know people who are quietly confident, who are comfortable whether in a starring or a supporting role. We want our egos to be like that second person.

All of this takes time and a great deal of courage. To demote the ego from the role of captain, to give up the idea that there is a self, and to meet everyone and everything without expectations or assumptions runs counter to everything we've learned about life. It can seem beyond frightening—it can seem dangerous. But the good news is that, when we let go of the illusions, our buddha-nature then becomes available to support us in ways our ego tried and failed to do.

As you can see, when I urge you to be committed to Zen, I don't just mean that you should do mind maps regularly or just that you should sit every day. (Although, of course, you should do mind maps, and you must sit every day!) Those things are vital, and sitting is the heart of the practice, but it is not mere consistency that I'm speaking of. I hope this book has made clear that the goal of Zen is nothing less than completely dismantling the delusions the self creates to feel unique, special, and separate from the rest of the world. To be committed to the project of waking up is to be committed to a complete reorientation of your life. It requires letting go of your delusion that you exist as a separate being. And it requires letting go of this delusion not just once but over and over again. I've mentioned before the three essential conditions a Zen student needs to wake up: great faith, great doubt, and great determination. Great faith is a belief that everyone has buddha-nature and that realization is possible, and it is necessary to have great faith in order to let go of the comforting delusion of the self. Great doubt is the ability to question what seems true. And to continue this questioning over and over, in order to keep sitting when you are frustrated, bored, angry, and even hopeless—that requires great determination.

When students first meet with me, I often tell them this is a warrior's practice, and it will be the hardest thing they ever do. But please don't be intimidated by this, because you already have everything you need to succeed and know everything you need to know. You are whole, perfect, and complete, just as you are! You just need to make a commitment to uncover your buddha-nature, and I hope this book has encouraged you in your journey.

APPENDIX A

Some Guidance on Zazen

IF YOU PICKED up this book and made it this far, I doubt you are a total beginner to meditation. And even if you are, there are a number of excellent works to help you begin a meditation practice.[15] Therefore, I do not intend to go step by step through the postures for sitting or how to create and maintain a practice. But I do have some suggestions and guidance to offer.

My first piece of advice is that if you want to practice seriously, if you want to change your life, you need to sit a lot—probably more than you think you have time for. You can no more gain surpassing clarity by meditating for fifteen minutes a day than you can look like a celebrity by exercising fifteen minutes a day. I am constantly telling my students to go sit more. Sometimes they get frustrated with me, but I've got evidence for my case. For centuries monks did almost nothing but sit—sometimes nine or ten hours a day—and it still took them years to wake up. Bodhidharma is supposed to have spent nine years in a cave staring at the wall—and that was after he'd chosen to bring the dharma to China! If you really want to wake up, don't make excuses; make time to sit at least twice a day, every day.

At the Zen center I founded, Soji, we teach beginners to follow their breath, which is the standard introduction for most types of meditation practice. Here I'd like to expand on that instruction, especially for those who do not have a teacher to work with.

IN-OUT BREATH FOCUS

This is what I recommend as a start—count the in-breath as "one," the out-breath as "two," and so on, up to ten. Then begin again at one. Counting the in- and out-breaths separately keeps your mind focused and makes it easier to notice when the mind wanders. If the mind does wander, go back to one rather than picking up where you were. Don't be discouraged if you spend an entire session vacillating between one and two or even if the sound of the ending bell makes you realize you didn't count at all. Don't judge yourself; just accept that your mind was distracted and refocus.

A useful tactic here is labeling your thoughts. Quietly making mental notes of what you find your mind doing—"planning," "dreaming," or even just "thinking"—can bring you back to your focus quickly because it suggests to the mind that this task is recognized and therefore done. As you become more practiced at letting go of thoughts, you can also let go of labeling, but it is an excellent guide back to the breath at first.

FULL BREATH FOCUS

The next step is to count "one" for an entire breath cycle, both in and out. Try not to focus too much on the counting—sometimes students report thinking, "Ooooonnnnee" through the whole breath or for the in- or out-breath. Instead, focus on the physical sensations and movements of the breathing itself and very quietly note, "One" at the end.

PURE BREATH FOCUS

When you feel confident in counting and can keep your focus much of the time, you should try dropping the counting and simply focusing on the breath itself. Keep your attention on the breath continuously, but without labeling or evaluating it. Just breathe and be present for the breath. Again, if (or, I should say, when) your mind gets bored or distracted and starts thinking, don't judge yourself. Simply return your attention to the breath.

SHIKANTAZA (JUST SITTING)

At this stage, you stop focusing on the breath or on anything at all and drop off body and mind. This is not something you try to do; you can't think your way to not thinking. In fact, you will first realize it has happened when you find yourself realizing that you were not thinking, which is of course the moment thinking reemerges.

This is a tricky moment, as you will be tempted to celebrate ("I was really in samadhi there!") or mourn ("I was there, and I blew it."). Either reaction creates a subject and object, a you that is meditating and a you that evaluates the success of that meditation. But don't blame yourself for having a reaction or a thought—that is, after all, what the mind does. Just return to your focus as smoothly as possible, without slipping into intellectualizing what just happened.

Remember that there is no goal in *shikantaza*, no good or bad sessions, because that would require evaluation and discrimination—the very mental states we are trying to let go of. If you spent an entire session fidgeting on your cushion, unable to get comfortable, that's what meditation was for you this time. If you drifted off into replaying an argument or planning your work week or fantasizing about a vacation, that's what meditation was for you this time. This is not to say you should passively accept whatever your mind offers. Zen meditation demands great determination, and you should make an effort to come back to your breath or your sitting each and every time you lose focus. But it will be best if you do it without judgment.

Finally, please don't think that once you have adopted one of the techniques, you can't go back to the "easier" or "beginner" techniques. All of these meditation exercises are available to you at all times, and while shikantaza may be closer to dropping all thoughts than is counting your breaths, that does not make it better.

KOAN STUDY

Taizan Maezumi Roshi, the founder of the lineage to which I belong, the White Plum lineage, received transmission (recognition of his realization and authority to teach) in both the Soto and Rinzai schools. Therefore, although I identify mainly as a Soto teacher, I use koan study, which is a Rinzai practice, with my students. Koan study can be a wonderful way to clarify the mind and gain insight beyond the intellect. It is also a powerful way to make sure you are really meditating and not just drifting. But koan study must only be undertaken with a teacher who has studied koans. Many people believe there are no right answers to koans or that whatever comes up for an individual practitioner is right. This is not true, although it is true that what comes up while sitting with a koan can be very instructive, especially about where you are stuck. But yes, there are "right" answers to koans, and it also is important to understand why that answer is the correct answer. Neither the answer nor the understanding can be verified by your own mind or a book; in this case, only a teacher will do.

Although I do not suggest trying to do traditional koan study on your own, sometimes it can be helpful to sit with a thought or phrase as a personal koan. The mind map questions, for example, can be excellent thoughts to drop into your sitting. Asking "Who am I?" or "What makes me angry?" can lead to some interesting results. However—and I cannot stress this strongly enough—*do not think* about your reactions. If posing the question "Who am I really?" makes you burst into tears, do not then ask yourself why or what's going on. Later you can journal or talk to a friend or see a therapist. While you are meditating, just cry. Just be present for that reaction, without judgment or evaluation. Be one with the reaction, and then be one with the moment the reaction ceases, and then, rather than clinging to the reaction ("What was that about?"), let the reaction drop off, along with body and mind.

One of the greatest powers of meditation is the promise you make to yourself that, for this set period of time, you will not get up and distract yourself from your feelings. The twenty or thirty or forty-five minutes of a sit are a container for strong emotions and reactions, a way to have them arise in a powerful way but also a way to gently let them go. Of course, as I noted back in the introduction, too much meditation, especially alone, can create mental loops and states that are not at all healthy, that can even be dangerous. If you find yourself dropping into a particular mental state each and every time you sit, find it impossible to let the mental state go, or find that you are meditating more and more because that is the only way you can cope, it is time to get off the cushion and seek professional help. And even if you are not having these difficulties, I urge you to find a group for at least some of your meditation practice. The three treasures, after all, are Buddha, dharma, and sangha, not Buddha, dharma, and sitting alone in your room. Even though the Buddha awakened on his own, he understood the profound importance of community, and we should as well.

APPENDIX B

I-System Terminology

Please be aware that this appendix only lists the terms used in this book. The full Mind-Body Bridging program involves several other aspects and methods of bridging. If you are interested in the full program, there are workbooks available from the Mind-Body Bridging Institute.

Bridging: This is a method to stop the harm caused by the overactive Identity-System. Bridging involves doing a map while focusing on the embodied present moment—tuning in to background sounds or feeling the floor under your feet—in order to make clear that the thoughts and feelings are not actually part of the present moment but instead are manufactured by the Identity-System.

Depressors: These help the Identity-System stay *on*. A depressor is the belief in a pattern—that a given incident fits into an overall pattern, and nothing will change. A depressor can be recognized by a "down" feeling, negative thoughts, and a heavy, tense body.

Executive Function: When the Identity-System is *off*, your Executive Function is in charge, regulating your mind to work in a relaxed and present manner. This is you at your best. This is you in your natural state.

Fixers: These help the Identity-System stay *on*. A fixer is the belief that change (of the self, the world, or both) is necessary for happiness. A fixer can be recognized by a sense of urgency, pushing you to do things because you feel bad. This pushing is the fixer.

Identity-System: Everyone has one. When your Identity-System is *on* (active), your mind clutter (spinning thoughts) and body tension get in the way of living a healthy life. They stop you from healing your trauma. When your Identity-System is *off* (resting), your mind is clear, and your body relaxed. Your body can now heal.

Mapping: Maps are short, pen-and-paper exercises where you jot down your thoughts and responses to a prompt or a personal feeling or experience. You then evaluate the body tension and mind clutter to see which of the thoughts are most powerful. Mapping allows you to separate your ideas from your self, to see that they are not fundamentally you.

Natural functioning: Natural functioning is recognized by how you act when you feel settled. This is how the brain functions when your Executive Function is in control.

Requirements: These are the things that can turn *on* your Identity-System. Requirements are thoughts and/or rules in your mind about how you and the world should be. You recognize them by the fact that you get upset when these rules are broken.

Story line: These keep the Identity-System going. A story line works to explain everything that happens in a way that makes individual events or feelings fall in line with your requirements. It is recognized by getting caught up in thoughts or stories that pull you away from the world and what you are doing in the present moment.

NOTES

1. John Welwood, *Toward a Psychology of Awakening* (Boston: Shambala Publications, 2000), 5.

2. M. Kathleen B. Lustyk, Neharika Chawla, Roger S. Nolan, and Alan Marlatt, "Mindfulness Meditation Research: Issues of Participant Screening, Safety Procedures, and Researcher Training," *Advances* 24, no. 1 (2009): 20–30.

3. Robert Augustus Masters, "Spiritual Bypassing: Avoidance in Holy Drag," accessed March 1, 2018, http://robertmasters.com/writings/spiritual-bypassing/.

4. Herbert V. Guenther and Leslie S. Kawamura, *Mind in Buddhist Psychology: A Translation of Ye-shes rgyal-mtshan's "The Necklace of Clear Understanding,"* Dharma Publishing, Kindle Edition (Kindle Locations 386–392).

5. Amber L. Story, "Self-Esteem and Memory for Favorable and Unfavorable Personality Feedback," *Personality and Social Psychology Bulletin* 24, no. 1 (1998): 51–64.

6. For a fun but excellent explanation of this phenomenon (called "the backfire effect"), see "You're Not Going to Believe What I'm about to Tell You," *The Oatmeal,* http://theoatmeal.com/comics/believe.

7. Peggy McIntosh, "White Privilege: Unpacking the Invisible Knapsack," *Peace and Freedom Magazine* (July/August, 1989): 10–12.

8. Caroline Brazier, *Buddhism on the Couch: From Analysis to Awakening* (Berkeley, CA: Ulysses Press, 2003), 145.

9. More information about Block's work is available at the Mind-Body Bridging website, http://mindbodybridging.com/about-mbb/. Block has also published a number of workbooks, including *Mind-Body Workbook for Stress, Mind-Body Workbook for Addiction*, and *Mind-Body Workbook for PTSD*.

10. The full Mind-Body Bridging system includes questions specifically designed to explore fixers and depressors. Since this book combines the Abhidharma and I-System models, I chose to introduce only the basic questions; if you are interested in exploring fixers and depressors more, I recommend Stanley Block's workbooks, such as *Mind-Body Workbook for Stress*.

11. The full Mind-Body Bridging system includes questions specifically designed to explore story lines. Since this book combines the Abhidharma and I-System models, I chose to introduce only the basic questions; if you are interested in exploring story lines more, I recommend Stanley Block's workbooks, such as *Mind-Body Workbook for Stress*.

12. I am indebted to Chögyam Trungpa for my ideas about how we rationalize our psychological states, especially his book *The Myth of Freedom and the Way of Meditation* (Boston: Shambhala Publications, 2002).

13. Robert Augustus Masters, *Spiritual Bypassing: When Spirituality Disconnects Us from What Really Matters* (Berkeley, CA: North Atlantic Books, 2010), 194.

14. For a wonderful exploration of this, see Chögyam Trungpa, *Glimpses of Abhidharma: From a Seminar on Buddhist Psychology* (Boston: Shambhala Publications, 2001).

15. There are a number of good online guides—just make sure to search for "Zen meditation" rather than just "meditation" if you are interested in learning postures and techniques for zazen specifically. *Lion's Roar* just recently put together a special issue (available in book form)

entitled *How to Meditate*. Dōgen described zazen in "Zazengi: Rules for Zazen" in 1243, and very little has changed since then. The piece can be found in various published translations, including John Daido Loori, ed., *The Art of Just Sitting: Essential Writings on the Practice of Shikantaza* (Boston: Wisdom Publications, 2002). The modern classic of sitting for the Soto school is Shunryū Suzuki's *Zen Mind, Beginner's Mind* (Tokyo: Weatherhill, 1970), and he also includes instructions for sitting in *Not Always So: Practicing the True Spirit of Zen* (New York: HarperOne, 2009).